A CHINESE ETHICS FOR THE NEW CENTURY

A Chinese Ethics for the New Century

The Ch'ien Mu Lectures in History and Culture,
and Other Essays on
Science and Confucian Ethics

Donald J. Munro

The Chinese University Press

*A Chinese Ethics for the New Century: The Ch'ien
Mu Lectures in History and Culture, and Other Essays
on Science and Confucian Ethics*
By Donald J. Munro

© **The Chinese University of Hong Kong**, 2005

ISBN 962–996–056–7

THE CHINESE UNIVERSITY PRESS
The Chinese University of Hong Kong
SHA TIN, N.T., HONG KONG
Fax: +852 2603 6692
      +852 2603 7355
E-mail: cup@cuhk.edu.hk
Web-site: www.chineseupress.com

Printed in Hong Kong

For

Yanming An, Steven Angle, Alison Black,
Sin-yee Chan, Robert Eno, Chad Hansen, Jerome Hill,
Manyul Im, Y. K. Lo, David Moser, Lisa Rogers,
William Savage, Lance Stell, and Brook Ziporyn

Contents

Foreword

Ambrose Y. C. King

Professor Donald Munro's *A Chinese Ethics for the New Century* is the latest volume published in the time-honored Ch'ien Mu Lecture in History and Culture Series. The Ch'ien Mu Lecture was established in 1978 by New Asia College, The Chinese University of Hong Kong, with the purpose of preserving and promoting Chinese culture through lecturing and publication of the works of scholars of high achievement in various fields. I venture to think that Professor Munro surely had some sense of satisfaction to be invited as the prestigious Ch'ien Mu Lecturer in 2003 at New Asia College where in the 1960s he studied Chinese philosophy under the neo-Confucian scholar Tang Junyi. Professor Munro was then a very young man.

Professor Munro, now Professor Emeritus at the University of Michigan, has had a distinguished academic career for the past four decades. His first book entitled *The Concept of Man in Early China*, published in 1969, won acclaim in the scholarly community for its philosophical inventiveness and sinological sophistication. Then, in 1977 and 1988 respectively, the publication of his second book, *The Concept of Man in Contemporary China*, and his third book, *Images of Human Nature: A Song Portrait*, established him as a leading scholar in the field of Chinese philosophy and ethics.

Professor Munro's trilogy, now modern classics, take questions in philosophy, education and ethics as their core concerns, and focus singularly on the traditional Chinese theory of human nature. His systematic exposition of the deep-level structure of thought of the great Confucians, Mencius and Zhu Xi, hidden in their discourse on ethics are truly original and imaginative. I am particularly impressed by his sympathetic yet objective exploration of the Chinese ethical ideal and its potential contribution to world ethics. The remarkable scholarship of Munro's trilogy is intelligently and competently expounded by Professor Liu Xiaogan's excellent introduction, and I want to say that Professor Munro's inquiry of Chinese ethics is his life-long intellectual journey, which has been unceasing despite the fact that he chose to retire from The University of Michigan almost a decade ago.

Professor Munro's present volume is a powerful testimony to his ever enriching scholarship on his cherished topics of the Confucian concept of equality and the question of individual autonomy and their modern meaning. In his three lectures for the Ch'ien Mu Lectureship, Professor Munro's discussion of the Mencian legacy of naturally equal human nature has had a "biological turn"; he brings in new biological science perspectives to the discourse in Chinese ethics. In a convincing manner, he demonstrates that the Chinese idea of natural equality meshes in significant ways with emerging developments in Western ethics which have developed from findings of new biology, especially evolutionary biology and evolutionary psychology. To his inquisitive delight, he finds the works of Edward Q. Wilson and Steven Pinker and other evolutionary scientists have convergence with the Mencian principle that has endured so long in China. The Confucian position on an inborn nature is reinforced by the findings of contemporary evolutionary biology. The Confucians and biologists agreed not only that there is a human nature, but also share beliefs about its content. Professor Munro augments Mencius and Zhu Xi's position that "Loving one's kin is humanness," and that kinship love is natural and proper by showing that modern biologists also explain altruism as similarly derived from kinship love. He makes it abundantly clear that modern biologists share with the Confucians the fundamental position, of which this first is: Altruism begins in the family and spreads outward. The Confucian core ethical concept, *shu*, meaning reciprocal altruism, also finds good support in the works of Robert Trivers and other like-minded evolutionary biologists or psychologists. In short, in this new volume, while rejecting total biological determinism, Professor Munro successfully puts the Confucian theory of ethics on a scientifically informed biological basis. Professor Munro believes that "the ultimate foundation of ethics lies not in a supernatural being or realm, but in what the early Confucians called the original mind found in us all at birth, and today we would call biology." Through new findings of evolutionary biological sciences, Professor Munro is ever convinced that some of Confucian ethic is consistent with the actual human condition, and to him, this is key to the question of why Confucianism has endured for so long.

In my view, Professor Munro has made a good case that the Mencian idea of equal worth is a Chinese gift to ethics and the Confucian ethical principles are all the more relevant in the new century. And his advice to revise Zhu Xi's formulation, so as "to shift its basis from *tiandao* to biology" is worth to be taken heed of by Chinese ethicists who wish to join the international discourse on construction of world ethics based on our common biological nature.

Those who are familiar with Professor Munro's trilogy on Confucian philosophy of ethics will find this admirably written book a delight to read, a continuation of his trilogy as well as a new intellectual contribution. For me, hearing Professor Munro's masterful delivery of his new lectures was truly a treat, and my personal renewal of friendship with him at New Asia College since our last meeting at the Breckenridge Conference Center, Bowdoin College in York, Maine in June 1981 is indeed most pleasant and to be treasured.

Preface

The reader of these essays may ask to what extent the references to modern science represent new scientific knowledge. The best way to answer is to identify the areas in biology and neuroscience in which new information about human social behavior is rare, and those in which it steadily accumulates. There is very little data on gene-social behavior relations, although the relevance of the genes is not a question. Of the roughly 30,000 of them, half or more are expressed in human brain cells, so they have something to do with how the brain is designed and works in mammalian action. To say there is a genetic basis for something is not to say anyone knows what the connection is. Some scientists believe that it was not until 1997 that the first plausible article appeared on a gene for mammalian social behavior. It concerned mice that had had a gene removed, resulting in disinterest in social contact and neglect of keeping their whiskers trim.[1] One problem is that because genes code for proteins, not traits, one gene's proteins may be involved in many, many different traits, a phenomenon called pleiotropy. Another problem is that up to a hundred or more genes may interact in most behavior. And they also interact with the environment.

The genome lays out the brain circuitry, which can be modified by experience. This circuitry is involved in predispositions or tendencies to certain social behavior. Konrad Lorenz and the Oxford zoologist Niko Tinbergen were among the first to study behavior through a biologist's eyes. Lorenz treated behavior patterns as like organs that had evolved in the species as a means of survival.[2] These can be studied. In the following essays, the references that I and some scientists make to human nature refer to these patterns in humans and to their associated emotions. There is a steadily increasing amount of information about them available to brain scientists, aided by MRI and similar technology, and to some social scientists familiar with various cultures. Herein lies a distinction that helps carve out the currently rich lodes of information. There are brain networks involved in all human social activities. The relevant brain networks, the motivations and information-seeking in which they are involved, plus the environments where it all happens, belong to the *proximate* causes of behavior. There are patterns in the neural connections accessible to brain science, and patterns of behavior found in large numbers of the world's humans accessible to social scientists. The scientists treat the behavior patterns as evidence for a genetic basis, even if its precise nature is not known. The patterns may be identified in a species or in all mammals. For example, one account reads, "The fact that differences in male and female aggressive behavior are so uniform across so many different mammalian species makes it highly likely that this difference has a genetic basis."[3] Another such pattern is altruistic behavior, costly to the agent, that is usually directed to individuals to whom the altruist has some genetic tie, rather than randomly to targets in the species. Also, there is child-care giver bonding.

The increasingly rich lode of information about the patterns includes the efforts of brain scientists, such as the neurologist Antonio Damasio. Using MRI equipment and human subjects with varying kinds of brain damage, they can identify the brain systems that support ethical behavior (memory, decision-making, creativity).[4] And they can put a final stop to the Platonic legacy that moral reasoning, or any reasoning, can occur without the emotions playing a role. Plato's position was that reasoning can and should occur in the mind alone. The emotions, being bodily and impure, should never intrude into the domain of thinking. Descartes reinforced this idea in the early modern period by arguing that the mind has access to knowledge only if it operates apart from anything physical, making deductions from innate truths. In this Platonic/Cartesian approach, there is no acknowledgement of the emotions that motivate study or that may bias its findings and no place for sensory observations in experiments.

The proximate causes of social behavior also include biochemical factors. Among these are the neurotransmitters serotonin, linked to varying levels of aggressive behavior, and dopamine, linked to the sense of well-being.

In addition to the proximate causes, there are sometimes speculative but often powerful explanations as to why such patterns of behavior have evolved. These *evolutionary* or *ultimate* causes try to explain how such patterns of behavior contribute to the reproductive success of the individuals or groups in a species. The works on kin selection by William Hamilton and on reciprocal altruism by Robert Trivers offer convincing explanations about kin selection in acts of altruism and how it fosters gene survival.[5] In another case, Antonio Damasio may have a high degree of validity for his descriptions of the automated brain functions in the social emotions sympathy, shame, pride, and guilt. He may know from other scientists that dolphins, chimps, and cats also manifest those emotions. But his proposal about their evolutionary cause (staving off danger, helping the organism take advantage of an opportunity), may have less weight.[6]

There is an additional source of information about human social behavior that does not flow from any scientist. This is contained in the collective wisdom of thoughtful observers in the past. China has a twenty-five hundred year history of writers focusing on moral psychology and human nature. Many of the authors were acutely concerned with the workability of their theses, because as scholar-officials they had to apply the principles in the social control of the people for whom they had supposed parental responsibility. Thomas Bayes (1702–1761) is now known for his "Bayesian statistics," which gives weight to unobservable quantities. He said that a person often begins with a subjective probability as an answer to a question, based on prior beliefs. New data can be built into future, newly reformulated answers. So, calculating is a series of changing probabilities. Today, Bayesian statistics acknowledges that proposed answers to many of the world's crucial questions are not open to rigorous tests. There is not enough current controlled data. In such cases, knowledge that has been accumulated over time about what works may be assigned a certain weight. The historical texts in which Chinese theories of human nature are described have answers to questions and evidence for them. That evidence has some validity for questions about human social behavior, just as archaeological artifacts may. They may help us ask the right questions today when we have better tools to judge answers. So our empirical observations in such cases may include the study of pre-modern texts. I would offer as an example the two thousand year history of Chinese explorations of the role of imitation in human learning. Giacomo Rizzolatti's 1991 discovery of the role of "mirror neurons" in imitative action simply brings modern science into the discussion of a topic about which much else has long been known in China.

Introduction

Opening a New Frontier: Donald Munro's Research on the History of Chinese Philosophy[1]

Liu Xiaogan

Professor Donald J. Munro is Professor Emeritus at the University of Michigan. He is not only a noted philosopher and educator (he appears regularly in *Who's Who in America*), but also an accomplished sinologist. In his early years he earned a degree from the Philosophy Department of Harvard University and later a Ph.D. from Columbia University's Department of Chinese and Japanese, with work in the Department of Philosophy. Moreover, he was mentored by Liu Yuyun and Tang Junyi in Taiwan and Hong Kong. In Western academic circles of the late 1950s it was rare to encounter the likes of Munro's systematic training in Western thought combined with his solid sinological command.

As soon as Munro had completed his Ph.D. he took up teaching duties at Michigan, where he earned a Distinguished Service Award. He has been a professor in both philosophy and Asian languages and cultures. He has earned many prestigious fellowships and academic awards, including those from the Guggenheim Foundation, the Ford Foundation, the American Council of Learned Societies, and the National Academy of Sciences. He also traveled widely to deliver endowed lectureships at American and Canadian universities, including the University of Vermont, Trent University (Ontario), University of Washington, and Stanford, where he was invited, respectively, as the John Dewey Lecturer, Gilbert Ryle Lecturer, Fritz Lecturer and Evens-Wentz Lecturer.

He also served in several distinguished national academic organizations, including chairing the American Council of Learned Societies' Committee on Studies of Chinese Civilization, and serving on the Asia Society's Committee on China and Central Asia.[2]

FAMILY TRADITIONS AND PERSONAL CHOICES

Professor Munro was born into an academic family. His father's family had been educators for several generations. His father, Thomas Munro, was also a philosopher, who had been influenced by his era's reverence for science. He devoted himself to questions on the scientific transformation of aesthetics and was a prolific writer. His most important works include *The Arts and Their Interrelations*, *Evolution in the Arts*, and *Form and Style in the Arts*. Some of his work has been translated into Chinese and collected in Li Zehou's edited volume, *Translated Anthology of Western Aesthetics.*

After graduating from Harvard's Philosophy Department, Munro served as a naval officer. During his service there he received a letter of commendation from the Chief of Naval Operations, and one can imagine that had he continued in the Navy that career path would have taken him far. But in the end, his family traditions and his own interests pulled him away from the Navy to Columbia University for graduate studies.

But Munro did not want to remain in the safety of his family's intellectual waters. His family came from a strong European background, his father's side from Scotland, and his mother's France and Romania. The entire clan's special strength lay in European studies. To carve out and develop an independent specialty, Munro deliberately avoided the family tradition. Indeed, in the 1950s American attention had begun to turn to Asia, and he set out to find in Asia his area of research. Munro felt that Chinese philosophy had the most depth, was the richest, most complex, and most meaningful; in the end he selected China as the special area he would study.

The works for which Professor Munro has been recognized all concern the Chinese concept of human nature. His first volume appeared in 1969 and was entitled *The Concept of Man in Early China*; the second volume, published in 1977, was called *The Concept of Man in Contemporary China*; and the third, published in 1988, was *Images of Human Nature: A Sung Portrait*. Scholars like Munro who spend twenty to thirty years covering a focused topic from antiquity to the present are few and far between. What aroused such an overwhelming interest in the human nature question and kept him at steady research efforts to address such an enormous span of history? To answer this question, we must turn to his college experience.

When Munro studied at Harvard, he took a class with the famous behavioral psychologist B. F. Skinner. Skinner tried to use physics as the model for psychology and focused all his attention on observable and measurable responses by people to external stimuli. This approach had notable strengths but completely neglected internal activities like thought, emotion, or motivation. At that time, Munro was intrigued by the prospect of doing such precise research on this topic: this was truly using science in the study of human nature. It was from this that Munro initially discovered his interest in the question of human nature. But after studying both Western and Chinese writings on human nature, he began to doubt the usefulness of this approach. Whether Western or Chinese, definitions of the "human" all involved people's interior life—like the Western notion of motivation and the ability to choose and to reason, and Chinese ideas of the social emotions such as benevolence and righteousness. Munro began to realize that approaches such as Skinner's, viewing people to be like material particles in physics, was mistaken. This realization only heightened Munro's interest in researching human nature.

Science has come to color many endeavors, and there are many different methods by which one can carry out scientific research; physics does not represent the only type of science. In the end the method Professor Munro pursued was what Roger Trigg later called the true objectivity method,[3] that is, striving to capture the truth of the object of one's research. According to this principle, research into human nature or psychology absolutely cannot use the same method physicists use for studying inanimate matter. In fact, people who research humankind must start from some comprehensive notion of "what humans are" and their methods indeed should reflect this. Our assumptions about human beings should include their every aspect—like important social relations, complex behavioral motivations, and relevant historical background, from goal-oriented behavior and individual unpredictability to the ongoing changeability of relevant factors around the research object. Research about people must pay attention to their every characteristic; our assumptions about them should be as rich as possible, as rational and unbiased as possible. It should come as close as possible to describing people's original state. Only this method can be considered truly scientific.

Developments show that Munro's self-confidence and sense of mission have proved correct. He has achieved success in his chosen arena of study and career. His first book caused a great stir in the scholarly community. A. C. Graham, a fellow of the British Royal Academy and professor at London University said of his book, "This is a stimulating and original attempt to find new guide-lines in Chinese thought ... [The] book belongs to the small number of works in English on Chinese thought which are lucid and original enough to stimulate." University of Pennsylvania professor of Chinese philosophy Derk Bodde wrote, "The book is exceptional among studies of Chinese philosophy on several counts.... Its combination of disciplinary [philosophical] acumen with sinological competence raises the study of early Chinese thought to a new level of sophistication." The breadth of cited materials, clarity of analysis, and the reliability of Munro's handling of concepts earned him the recognition of the academic world. His second and third books were also hailed as benchmarks for future research, each full of questions, insights, and revelations. Any one who had seriously read his books had to acknowledge that the depth, breadth and great care taken in Munro's research gave each of his books a certain authority.

A UNIQUE PURSUIT AND EXPLORATION

A most important motivation for Munro's research into the history of Chinese philosophy was his interest in the basic patterns of Chinese thought. Munro was fascinated to discover the deep-level structures of thought hidden in discourse on ethics. These basic patterns and structures of thought were prior to and conditioned each and every Chinese philosophical exploration as well as the content and methods of education. Through them the numerous and complex results of these explorations and education take on a family resemblance and a common character over the course of Chinese history. Put another way, Munro has single-handedly tried to get at the most basic reasons why people think in a certain way. Of course, the reasons he points to are neither geographical nor historical; they are not topographical, climatic, class or conflict-related, or technological. Even though these factors are all important in human experience, what Munro has concerned himself with is why philosophers' theories and their defense of their mode of thinking all have a certain special form. His research on Zhu Xi highlights the structural nature of images extracted from things commonly seen and thoroughly familiar in daily life, for instance, running water, the family, plants, and so forth. He discovered that many Chinese and Western theories are similarly built on such images or metaphors.

Trying to uncover the reasons behind phenomena was an extension of his primary motivation in researching Chinese ideas of human nature. He notes that any important theory, no matter if it concerns the individual or society, is always based on a particular view of human nature. This is true for the ancient period and today. Contemporary humanities (literature, philosophy, art, and language) and the social sciences (economics, psychology, sociology, and political science) are no different. For instance, many contemporary Western economists believe that individuals are motivated by self-interest and use this as a basic factor for explaining human behavior. Moreover, they hold that the best method for social science research takes as its standard individuals who rationally follow their self-interest. In contrast, sociologists emphasize that when we consider individuals as members of a group the special signs of their mutual relationships persist. Munro handles the history of Chinese thought the same way: that is, among distinctive Chinese thinkers he traces out clearly or not-so-clearly expressed differences in their theories of human nature; other content is worked out from this. In the twentieth century, many famous Chinese thinkers welcomed the Western values or concepts of democracy and equality, but their understanding and explanations of these concepts clearly carried the stamp of Wang Yangming's thinking. Even the likes of Sun Yat-sen (Sun Zhongshan), Li Dazhao, and Xiong Shili—all highly varied thinkers—were deeply influenced by Wang's concept of conscience or innate knowledge of the good (*liangzhi*). This demonstrates how a traditional Chinese theory of human nature worked, as it had for centuries, through fresh investigations of the human condition in modern China.

Some scholars make small distinction between themselves as individuals and as scholars. Professor Munro, however, has sorted out the roles of person and scholar very clearly. As a scholar, his research seeks to put aside his individual feelings of like and dislike, and, to the greatest extent possible, pursue problems objectively. But as an individual he cannot but have his own preferences. Munro's other, more personal motivation in his research into the history of Chinese philosophy is to discover and promote things of value in the long Chinese tradition, and on occasion to inspire other people. In this respect he may give rise to controversy, first because certain Chinese scholars have taken a condemnatory attitude toward their own cultural traditions, and also because what foreign scholars have praised and criticized in Chinese culture has differed from person to person. But as a Westerner who studies Chinese culture, when Munro praises or takes something to task his reasons for doing so in the end prove insightful and significant for any Chinese scholar who has thought deeply about them.

Munro notes that Confucius' observations on the mutual relations between social actors can make us recognize that we have special duties and obligations toward others, that we should not, as Western utilitarian and Kantian thinkers do, advocate that all people should be treated as the same kind of item.[4] When the Chinese are in the midst of pursuing equality and "universal love," how can they advocate the Confucian love that recognizes social and class differences? Actually, Confucian theories had recognized and generalized from the universal phenomenon of different levels of affection and affirmed its reasonableness. In fact, very few people have ever truly been able to achieve love that does not recognize differences. If one treated one's parents like strangers, and treated a woman one did not know the same as one's own wife, what sort of a world would it be? The Confucian principle of treating kin like kin and Western equality and universal love are argued from completely different levels. Throwing them together or comparing them is of course incorrect (and of course, Confucians did not entirely lack the concept of universal love). In his consideration of the Daoists, Munro sees the nonhuman natural world—its plant, animals, and rivers—like the human world—worth valuing and nurturing. To make a physical demonstration of this thinking, Munro and his wife and friends built a large cabin in the woods of northern Michigan. There he and family members act as nature's stewards, giving back to the great outdoors, and in the process gaining much pleasure.

Combining the historical and the philosophical

Munro's particular pursuit meant that his research would be different from others' in many respects. First, his work manifests a strong combined historical and philosophical bent. Most scholars focus on problems in one or two periods—pre-Qin, Wei-Jin or Song-Ming—and select one or several problems or figures from these periods on which to do research. Munro, however, has explored the Chinese concept of human nature and values in the key periods of the pre-Qin, Song, and contemporary times. Munro's research is clearly historical and powerfully theoretical as well. Its historical basis is expressed in how he handles the expression and development of concepts and topics in different historical periods, an effort that exhibits the sensitivity and care of a historian. His three volumes on Chinese theories of human nature taken together have the characteristics of a general history. His theoretical interest is expressed in the fact that each of these three books takes questions in philosophy, education, and ethics as its core concern, rather than being devoted to tracing development of a historical figure or thought. Munro pays special attention to Chinese ideas about people and their views of value. This is especially so where he considers the relationship between educational values and how individuals achieve maturity. Munro suggests that Confucian theories of human nature come together in the view that people's minds are innately things that evaluate. This view is the basis of the notion that people can, through self-cultivation and social education, achieve moral perfection. An outstanding characteristic of Chinese culture is its emphasis on the active participation of the individual and the state in early education. In one respect this expresses active encouragement of individual self-cultivation; in another respect it legitimizes the state's penetration of people's thinking and how knowledge is imparted, from which it achieves all-powerful control. These views of Munro's are original and the result of the combining historical research and theoretical analysis. Purely historical inquiry or purely theoretical discussions would be hard-put to arrive at such a conclusion.

A comparative approach

Munro's systematic training in Western philosophy has put him in a strong position to carry out comparative studies of Chinese and Western thought. He pays close attention to the methods Chinese and Western thinkers use to solve problems and the distinct development of their thought. Thus, Zhu Xi, St. Augustine, and Descartes, when discussing the concept of the innate mind, all use the metaphor of light. Some Western scholars hold that it is not appropriate or even possible to make a comparison between these philosophers. One cannot translate between one culture's system of thought and another's. Some believe that making a Chinese-Western comparison will decentralize the topic of discussion. Munro believes that so long as concrete cultural differences are pointed out, this sort of comparison can be helpful in deepening our comprehension of philosophers' thinking, for understanding questions of concern in Chinese and foreign cultures and why cultures sooner or later take up or give up one stream of thought or another. For instance, take metaphors for heaven: European philosophers used the sun as an image for God and believed people's innate mind was the result of God directly entering people's hearts with His light. But people had to experience this sort of knowledge to establish a connection with God. This problem was their greatest concern. Zhu Xi, however, did not worry over the vertical relation between people and God, but rather the horizontal relationship that links all things. Zhu Xi believed that the principle of self-knowledge in people's minds would help them realize those links and fervently care for things outside themselves. Clearly Zhu Xi's concerns differed from those of Western philosophers. When making such comparisons, Munro pays close attention to the differences in cultural background. For instance, when he touches on Western and Chinese individualism, Munro makes a point of noting that individualism as we know it is in fact a modern Western concept of the nineteenth century, that it originated when German Romantic artists and poets began to take seriously and emphasize the self. Thus Munro makes readers mindful of the differences between the concepts of recent Western philosophers and Chinese thinkers of antiquity. He fully exploits his training in Chinese and Western philosophy to provide the necessary background knowledge as he makes these comparisons.

Objectivity and the sense of accuracy

Another characteristic of Munro's work is its objectivity and fine degree of accuracy. He is not satisfied to elucidate the internal consistency of a few theories, and pays more attention to the consistency between different thinkers and schools. Examples include the similarity of the Daoist and Confucian concepts of human nature, and convergences in the concepts of mind/heart (*xin*) in Confucianism and Mao Zedong thought. Because he studies Chinese ideas of persons in general, a problem that is both basic and comprehensive, it would be easy for his work to slip into mediocrity or shallowness. But Munro has avoided this pitfall by relying on careful discipline and scholarly sophistication. He uses a great number of antecedents from antiquity, modern China, and elsewhere to elucidate his views. This way he is able to take what seem extremely common problems and transform their consideration into an infinitely fine-grained study. In his analysis, he is a scientific believer in facts, firmly supporting what he says with many facts and not allowing his assertions to exceed the allowable scope of objective evidence. He has never done the type of research that asserts absolute conclusions, but rather has unceasingly worked to increase the strength of his historical and theoretical explanations. Munro also pays much attention to maintaining a sympathetic attitude as he comes to understand and analyze different thinkers. But he does not play the part of advocate for any one thinker. He is good at revealing the persuasiveness and appeal of all sorts of philosophical and cognitive styles, at the same time clearly pointing out theoretical gaps and moral failures. Munro represents the spirit of classic liberalism; this means the objectivity and tolerance to work through another's terminology to comprehend that other thinker, and beyond that, the serious-mindedness to reveal the conditions under which such thinking about other people's thought, behavior, and position in society may create unforgivable constraints. This attitude and a subtle sense of accuracy are interrelated. Even though Munro is entirely careful to reveal and provide evidence for modes of thought claiming that universalism lies behind phenomena, he has never claimed that this model proves what determines the development of things; he does not say that conclusions of his own research into theories of human nature point to what absolutely determine any particular results in Chinese thought and education. Rather, he only emphasizes that these models can significantly explain a fairly broad sweep of philosophical and educational phenomena. This not only demonstrates an objective and cautious scholarship, it also manifests the accomplishment of mature judgment based in his subtle sense of accuracy.

From the characteristics described above, Munro's research gains another aspect, that is, attention to the precision and clarity of concepts. This is tied to the training in Western philosophy he received at Harvard and Columbia. He deliberately took the strong points, the stress Western philosophy attaches to analysis and definiteness of concepts, and applied them to his study of Chinese philosophy. He crafted clear definitions for each concept he used, and for a Chinese philosophical term that had complex and ambiguous meanings, he paid attention to explaining and analyzing them point by point. This is especially necessary when studying the history of Chinese philosophy, since so many philosophers of antiquity were fond of teaching by analogy to demonstrate their points. There are many instances where a given graph takes on several meanings, and different philosophers used the same term differently, but did not specify an explanation or a definition. This is most inconvenient for modern readers.

Chinese philosophers of the ancient period rarely displayed logical deduction. They did not often give definitive explanations of their propositions or assumptions. The complex significance of their propositions must usually be sorted out from the context of their discussion. Munro is extremely careful to look into the concrete implications of the ancient thinkers' propositions, and gives the reader a solid and detailed explanation. His work is not at all like the common attitude, presenting a vague spiritualism or ordinary observations about moral intuition. His conclusions about the self-evident truths that are the foundation of philosophical thought are always specific and clear, couched in narratives that can be tested. His concepts, such as "descriptive equality," "the mind/heart cluster," "malleability," "the power of models," and "the universality of human nature" are each a case in point; they all demonstrate his tremendous efforts in this area. Below we introduce some of these important concepts as a window into his work.

TWO KINDS OF EQUALITY: A CONSIDERATION OF ANCIENT CHINA

In his first book, Munro revealed an important point that had never received much notice before: namely, the concept of "natural equality" in early Chinese philosophy. It is generally believed that both Confucians and Legalists supported and protected a class system which held that people's functions and positions in society were different. Therefore it is rare to find a concept of equality that is dominant in the history of Chinese thought. Munro, however, points out that while ancient Chinese did not have the modern Western idea of equality, a number of ideas of descriptive or natural equality did hold sway. The crux here is that Munro was the first to distinguish between what he terms descriptive and evaluative equality. These are broadly significant and vastly different concepts. Modern Western equality is evaluative and implies that all people inherently have the same value (of course the concrete contents of "value" are various). They therefore should receive the same level of treatment, for example, the same political or economic rights, the same status before the law, and so forth. On this score, traditional Chinese philosophers held that people (meaning mainly adults) realized different levels of achievement in society and so treating them unequally was reasonable. What so-called descriptive equality means then, is that all human life inherently has the same factual nature, that is, the same original nature or particular qualities. This is the kind of equality meant by the term "natural equality." It is the equality people have before they mature in society and assume a certain social role. One of Munro's research topics focuses on the relationship between this Chinese descriptive equality and the notion of human nature in the history of Chinese thought.

There are many basic differences between the concepts of evaluative and descriptive equality, but this does not mean that they lack areas where they coincide. Sometimes evaluative aspects can be attached to declarations about the descriptive nature of human equality. One instance Munro gives is that people are naturally good. This is adding the evaluative concept of goodness to a "descriptive" natural state. St. Augustine thought that some people had a greater talent for reasoning than others, and so were more "good." Munro, like St. Augustine, seems to make a judgment about this "descriptive" natural state, but in fact there are important differences between these two assertions. Any statement about the descriptive nature of equality (or inequality) must emphasize the attributes of people's natural endowments, and any implications of an evaluative nature are secondary.

Furthermore, in Chinese evaluative statements, the quality of "goodness" in people differs from both "value" and "nobility." When Mencius talks about human nature as "good," he emphasizes that it is the potential people are born with, and not the characteristic of a typical adult. So-called goodness means that in a fixed and appropriate environment people's future actions very likely will be in harmony with their needs and will fall within the scope of customary behavior. But, in Western evaluative statements value and nobility always represent characteristics "heaven" bestows on people, which belong to them in perpetuity; they in no way refer to any possible, hoped for behavior. Finally, descriptive statements do not necessarily include the idea that people should receive any particular sort of treatment, only generalized "nurture." Mencius asserted that when people are born, their basic nature is good, but this does not imply that all people should receive just and unbiased treatment. Nor does it imply that adults should have equal rights. Thus, in Western evaluative statements of equality, the first thing emphasized is that people should be treated fairly and should enjoy equal rights over the course of their entire lives.[5]

The concept of natural equality was the product of and weapon with which thinkers of the Spring and Autumn and Warring States periods opposed aristocratic society's hereditary control. Ancient China's many philosophers did not consider hereditary status the only standard for official promotion. Confucius never believed that the rank a person was born into should decide his lifelong social position. His principle was "with education there is no distinction between students" (*youjiao wulei*), and among his students there was no lack of men of outstanding ability who had been born lowly but came to achieve recognition in society. Confucius stressed that "by nature, men are really alike; by practice they become different,"[6] recognizing that people's differences are most importantly the result of environmental influences. Mencius went a step further to argue and prove that all people are born with the four moral qualities of benevolence, righteousness, proper rituals and wisdom, that sages and ordinary people have the same basic nature. Thus, "the sage and I are of the same sort."[7] Xunzi clearly indicates that even among the descendant of kings, princes, or ministers, if one cannot comply with the regulations of ritual and ceremony, then he should return to the common people. And when descendants of commoners are able to respectfully abide by the rites, when their studies have come to fruition and their comportment and behavior is proper, they should be elevated to the aristocratic ranks.[8] Mozi advocated universal love and honoring the worthy: "The sage kings of ancient times ranked the virtuous high and honored the worthy, and although a man might be a farmer or an artisan from the shops, if he had ability, they promoted him.... Then no official was necessarily assured of an exalted position for life, nor was any member of the common people necessarily condemned to remain forever humble."[9] The Legalists Shang Yang and Han Fei advocated that law should rule the state: "The law does not fawn on the noble," and "punishment for fault never skips ministers; reward for good never misses commoners."[10] Daoists do not talk about the goodness of human nature, but do say that the simple naturalness with which people are born should not be harmed, and any regulated social behavior may harm this natural original humanity. Whether something is good or bad, noble or debased, from the Daoist viewpoint it is all the same. Daoists are the most thorough theorists about natural equality.[11]

From the big picture we can see that thinkers in ancient China rarely stress *a priori* high and low, noble and mean; in this sense, the endlessly debating Confucians, Mohists, and Daoists were unusually unified, and this unity has by and large extended to modern China. Of course, China has no lack of traditions about "winning a noble position and giving prestige to wife and children" (*fengqi yinzi*) or clever sayings like "Dragon bears dragon, phoenix bears phoenix, the mouse's children can all dig holes." There is also the common feeling among the elderly that "if our children take over our work, we can rest easy." This is perhaps why we rarely think about equality as a dominant concept in China. But if we look at it closely, thinkers in ancient China who argued successfully that high/low, noble/base were the original categories for human beings were very few, or at least they were not paid much attention. It is a shame that this view has for so long been obscured by the traditions and practices of the patriarchal clan system and overlooked by the scholarly world.

Concepts of equality: East and West

Ancient Chinese concepts of natural and biological equality have been extremely significant for political and social movements; they also impart to Chinese culture important differences from Western culture. Plato insisted on the view that some people's souls were better than others, and categorized souls as being of the gold, silver, or bronze class, with the distinction corresponding to the three levels of reason, spirit, and desire and to the three classes of rulers, warriors, and peasant-artisan-merchants. Plato never completely dismissed the idea of natural equality, but he believed that it had only existed in the remote past; that is to say, at the world's creation all souls had once been equal, but thereafter irreversible changes had occurred. For Plato, the rotten part of the human body was the slave of the healthy part, the flesh was the slave of the soul. Just the same, people whose souls were too closely constrained by the flesh were slaves of people whose souls' reason had mastered the flesh. Aristotle also held that people's natures were not the same. Many people were by nature slaves. Not only did slaves have no citizens' rights, neither did artisans, merchants, shepherds, women and serfs enjoy the status of citizens. Because they had no deliberative faculty, these types of people could not serve any function in government matters. The views of Plato and Aristotle and those of the Confucians are clearly different. In the thinking of the Confucians, the natural superiority of heaven versus earth, and yang versus yin was not so strongly extended to humanity's original condition. This distinction had an important and lasting impact on the long-term development of Chinese philosophy.[12]

The West did not completely lack the concept of natural equality. The ancient Greek Sophist Antiphon asserted that Greeks and barbarians shared the same natural endowments and so should be treated the same. A student of Gorgias said, "God set all men free, Nature has made none a slave." However, these positions were not widely held among Greek philosophers. Ideas of biological or natural equality for the Stoics became relatively powerful. The Stoics held that reason and God were of the same stuff and were immanent in all things. Because all people have the innate ability to reason, so they are naturally equal. Cicero said, "There is nothing else so clearly like people as other people. People are just alike in their basic nature." Some say the Roman "Law of the peoples" was heavily influenced by the Stoics. However, they themselves did not make great efforts to put their ideas into practice.

In Judaism and early Christianity, equality was from the first evaluative. Judaism preached that all people are equal before the laws of God, and Christianity promoted the equal value of all God's children; all of humanity has the hope of achieving equality in salvation. St. Paul said to the Galatians, "There is neither Jew nor Greek, there is neither bond nor free, there is neither male nor female; for ye are all one in Christ Jesus." This sort of equality is not natural equality. It is an equality based on the belief that God recognizes the equal value of all His children; it does not imply that all people possess the same positive qualities they were born with. True, the Christian doctrine that all people possess souls provides a basis for the idea of natural equality, and in fact, clearly from the beginning a minor thread in common Christian thought emphasized this equality, opposing Plato and Aristotle's classical legacy. But this did not change the fact that the concept of natural inequality remained dominant in the West up to the recent past. Therefore, when Descartes noted that people are naturally equal, because people all equally possess the light of reason, his view was considered provocative and revolutionary. In the West, Plato's teachings made people believe that there exists in the universe a natural class system and therefore they were to accept the class system in human society. People were born unequal. St. Augustine went a step further to strengthen this theory: "From heaven to earth, from the visible to the invisible, some things are good, others better than others. In this they are unequal, so all kinds of things might be."

Chinese descriptive equality

Since natural equality is extremely important in China, and comparatively unimportant in the West, why should the democratic politics based on an assumption of equality have emerged from Europe and not China? This is a very tough question to answer satisfactorily, but one fact is clear. The equality that Chinese stress focuses on the condition of people at birth, so the moral imperative rests, theoretically, on attributes that are experiential. This way of thinking suggests that the state should support an educationally and economically nurturing environment, so that each person is able to develop into a moral person, but on the question of how adults should be treated it is silent. This notion of equality and the phenomenon of inequality in social status and political rights never come into direct conflict, nor does natural equality have a point of contact with the idea or system of special privilege. Privileges can and should be given to people who are of outstanding moral quality.

In the West the idea of equality has seen its most important change in the step-by-step development of its evaluative sense. Martin Luther's religious Reformation was clearly instrumental in this. The equality factor was especially stressed and brought to bear in early Christianity. The Reformation movement produced a new concept, that is, in God's eyes all people have the same worth, and so should enjoy some common political power. Locke believed that from the perspective of experience, people are in fact not equal. His idea, "all men are created equal" does not speak to people's natural characteristics, but rather points to their value in the eyes of God. Therefore no one is born with the right to rule other people, but all people should receive fair and just treatment. People retain their equal value throughout their lives, and only those few who are "approved" command the qualification to rule others. Following from this idea is a sort of logical demand: if someone is not able to give others evenhanded, unbiased treatment, or does not recognize others' equal rights, he must give a definite reason why. On the other hand, when equality is referred to only in its descriptive sense, then it carries no implication of evaluative equality—that the ruler must gain the consent of the ruled, or that the individuals all should get fair treatment or enjoy equal rights.

The importance of the concept of natural equality lies not only in its revealing an important divergence between Chinese and Western cultures, but also in its serving as the foundation of several basic concepts in China. Because Chinese believe that when people are born they are all alike, with no defect, and each and every one of them through education can reach a state of moral perfection, so the educational environment and educational methods can decide a person's moral quality. Thus, education reform is commonly considered key in resolving social crises or political problems. Related to this is the continued importance of traditional educational content and method in modern theories of education and social control. The basic goal of education and self-cultivation is to firmly establish the parameters of correct behavior, that is, to enable the individual to internalize social controls. The best way to achieve this goal is to set up models, and so it is said "the power of models is infinite."

Professor Munro points out that this practice has historical roots. The premodern civil service examinations and the contemporary "Three Peoples' Principles" (*Sanmin zhuyi*) and Marxist education all have been used as basic avenues to resolve social problems. In areas led by the Guomindang (Kuomintang), university faculty included military training officers, in Communist-led areas education at all levels included political leadership workers. After 1949, the mainland experienced wave after wave of thought struggle movements or political study movements—all to resolve the problem of educating all citizens. After the political gale of the spring of 1989, the Communists' practical actions centered on resolving or keeping the lid on social contradictions through economic development, but their conclusion as to why the political storm had occurred was that the Marxist education given to young people had grown slack. Thus, once again the party promoted a movement to study Mao's work and learn from Communist models such as Lei Feng, a young soldier who died from an accident, and Jiao Yulu, a party cadre who died of disease. Party leaders seemed to believe that as long as Marxism is inculcated in the youth of generation after generation, the political power of the "proletariat" would be forever secure.

In China's ancient theories of human nature, Professor Munro identified a new explanation for social phenomena and the thrust of education in contemporary Chinese society; he ferreted out from Chinese tradition key deep-level reasons for the great emphasis Chinese put on education. This is truly admirable. But here we must also point out that what early Chinese tradition emphasized in education was respect for Confucius, studying the classics, and the Confucian principles of ethics. What some modern society's leaders have considered important in education is communist ideology and Marxism. Anyone can carry out this kind of education; there is no need for much preparation or expense. The Communist leadership does not take seriously enough a modern education in the sciences and humanities, one that would take greater investment. They tend to dismiss modern humanities and social science education as so much capitalist theory. This is a key reason why in China, although there is a longstanding tradition of valuing education, yet the state's level of education outlay, as well as teachers' social position has all along been maintained at the world's lowest level. It is only in the past decade that this situation has seen dramatic improvement.

THE MAOIST AGE AND TRADITIONAL CLUSTERING

Munro undertakes many different creative analyses of Chinese philosophical history, and applies them in his analysis of modern China. Here I would like to cite the idea of clustering from his second book, *The Concept of Man in Contemporary China*, as an example.

Clustering is Munro's term for an aspect of the Confucian and Maoist concept of mind (or social nature). It provides a justification not only for the kind of government that should exist but also for the manner in which that government should exercise its duties.

Clustering involves a combination of three mental phenomena: knowing, feeling, and promptings to act (motives). Knowing involves both understanding the distinctions between things in the natural world that correspond to distinctions marked by language and recognizing moral principles. Some of these distinctions are regarded by the Chinese as normative. In the past, they were regarded as Nature's signals as to what object or course of acton is superior or inferior, right or wrong, or proper or improper.

Feelings are concomitant with the act of recognizing (knowing) and of acting in accordance with what is known. Joy, anger, pity, and so forth always accompany knowing. Evaluations are also contained in these emotions. Certain feelings, such as joy, convey approval, others disapproval. Thus evalution can arise either from the act of knowing or the act of feeling. In Chinese tradition, there is a blurring of the distinction between the mind's recognition of factual distinctions and its making evaluations. There is no factual knowledge that does not contain a potential association with an evaluation.

Finally, the prompting to act in a certain manner is relevant to knowing or feeling. Because they assume the probability of association between "knowing" and "promptings to act," educated Chinese have always been sensitive to the behavioral implications of a principle or theory. They assume that once people learn a principle, they will be inclined to behave in a certain way.[13]

Traditional clustering of mind

Confucian concern with this "consciousness cluster" included as their first item knowledge (or cognition). Ancient Confucians considered "righteousness" (a moral component) and "knowing" as the main functions of the mind, so their "mind" in fact was a value judging mind.

Their so-called "knowing" meant grasping general moral principles—as one would distinguish facts from the natural world, one distinguishes what is morally correct and incorrect. The "knowing" of the later Song and Ming Confucianists can be divided into three types. The first is sensory knowing, stemming from direct experience of stimuli that affect the senses. The other two forms of knowing involve understanding principles (*li*). One involves grasping principles by intuition or by inference from a number of cases. The other kind of moral knowing involves being able to determine whether a particular thing is abiding by rules contained in the principles. These last two types of knowing are both closely identified with moral knowledge and value judgment. In the Confucian theory of knowledge, sensory and moral knowledge are often closely connected, but moral knowledge is more heavily weighted. Just as Wang Yangming said, "Innate knowledge does not come from hearing and seeing, and yet all seeing and hearing are functions of innate knowledge."[14] This moral knowledge is clearly higher than and prior to sensory knowledge.

The second item in the Confucian consciousness cluster is the emotions. Mencius said, "Reason and righteousness please my heart in the same way meat pleases my palate."[15] "Pleasure" is a sort of happy emotion, and here it expresses two levels of thought. First, moral knowledge or judgment, like sensory knowledge, occurs naturally; second, it expresses approval for appropriate, correct, or good behaviors, just as dislike expresses a negative judgment. The pre-Qin Confucians and Song-Ming idealists both frequently used the technical expression "sense of right and wrong." This refers to using right and wrong for distinguishing an object, and expresses the content of this theory of knowledge, at the same time "right" implies approval and support, "wrong" implies negation and opposition. Thus, both of these have an emotional color. The saying "sense of right and wrong" always signifies the simultaneous functions of cognitive distinguishing and emotional judgment. Wang Yangming noted, "Innate knowledge is nothing but the sense of right and wrong, and the sense of right and wrong is nothing but to love [the right] and hate [the wrong]. To love [the right] and hate [the wrong] covers all senses of right and wrong, and the sense of right and wrong covers all affairs and their variations."[16] This recognizes that cognitive activity and emotional experience nearly always take place simultaneously. Wang also says, "Seeing beautiful colors appertains to knowledge, while loving beautiful colors appertains to action. However, as soon as one sees that beautiful color, he has already loved it. It is not that he sees it first and then makes up his mind to love it."[17] This points to the unity of the process of knowing and emotional activity.[18]

From this unity of cognitive process and emotional activity we can infer two conclusions. First, by recognizing a moral principle an individual in effect accepts it, and emotional approval implies acceptance. Second, the mind always possesses the ability to project emotion to matters beyond the individual person, and this emotion can elicit actions that will affect others. When this emotion is unobstructed it can affect a person's status within his or her social network. This fact means that the Confucian concept of mind stands in clear contrast to an aspect of the idea of a "private" mind in the West, where the separation and independence of people's minds from state or group control are stressed.

The third item in the Confucian clustering is the compounding of the intention to act and knowledge. This points to the subjective origins of behavior, the subjective impulse that when unobstructed will gather force to proceed from the heart outward and develop into behavior. So the compounding of knowledge and the intention to act is not the same as Wang Yangming's "unity of knowledge and action." In this latter formula, "action" more frequently refers to publicly observable acts. The compound formulation can be traced back to the *Great Learning*: "This is the meaning of the expression 'when there is sincerity within, it will be expressed externally.'" This stresses the necessary connection between the activities of the mind and the intention to act. It expresses the concept "righteousness" in the Confucian sense of morality, and its demand for a high rate of correspondence between the inner activities of the mind and an individual's behavior. "Righteousness" not only means distinguishing the appropriate from the inappropriate; it also extends this judgment to behavior. For Confucians, the mind is usually the regulator of internal rules and the commander of external actions; this is a result of internalizing ruling power. Confucians also divide knowledge into two levels: shallow and deep; the deeper the knowledge, the more likely the intention to act will be carried forward into public action. So Cheng Yi says, "When knowing is deep, then action in accord with it will necessarily be perfect. There is no such thing as knowing what should be done and not being able to do it. Knowing and not being able to act is only a sign that the knowing does not go deep."[19] This knowing concerns the recognition of "truth," and the deeper that becomes, the higher the likelihood of the correctness of one's actions. This is of a piece with

Socrates' "moral knowledge, moral actions," though Socrates considers ignorance the source of evil, while Confucians see it in private desires deceiving the mind. So the depth or shallowness of knowing follows from and changes according to the degree of deception.

Some contemporary Chinese thought was influenced by classical Marxism and Soviet thought, so the contemporary "consciousness cluster" differs in some ways from the traditional version. But both believe in the close bond between mental activities such as cognition, emotion, and the intention to act; in this respect the contemporary and ancient formulations are the same.

Maoist clustering

In Maoist China the foremost aspect of the clustering is the intimate relationship between cognition and the emotions. Mao Zedong once said that knowledge determined the innate character and patterns of affairs, and so theoretically cognition and the emotions must be separated. But in reality, for contemporary Chinese cognition and the emotions are always bound up with each other. There is no cognitive activity that is not accompanied by a positive or negative emotional response. As expression of a knower's attitude, emotions will always return to the object of knowledge. So Chinese psychology textbooks say emotions are produced as knowledge becomes conscious, and moreover, they will change as knowledge changes. For instance, we know how great our own country is, and this will produce feelings of intense patriotism. As what we know about our country increases, our patriotism will grow deeper. In the vocabulary of Chinese Marxism, the class-bound formulation of emotions reflects the principle of many linked psychological activities. Mao Zedong said, "In a class society every person occupies a certain class position, and there is no thought that does not bear the stamp of class."[20] This assertion that all thought bears the stamp of class implies two things. First, because a person always lives within a certain class grouping, carrying out a certain kind of work, her thinking will assume a certain form. Second, people's class consciousness governs their psychological activity. Thus, all sorts of psychological activities can be grouped together according to classist principles. Emotion is not only connected to knowledge, it also goes together with value judgment. For instance, liking the color red is not only a kind of emotion, it also brings together positive judgments about the things red symbolizes. Chinese philosophers and psychologists all assert that there is no pure emotion. This explains why in the "consciousness cluster" of the mind there can never not be emotional factors, and in fact, emotion is the carrier of value judgments. And just as in the Confucian "consciousness cluster," the emotion that accompanies a particular piece of knowledge is not always necessarily correct. It is up to the individual to ensure that the accompanying emotion will be correct.

A second aspect of clustering in the Maoist period is the linking of cognition and action. That is to say, the tendency of an individual to act on a particular matter and his knowledge of and value judgment about the matter are always closely linked. This reflects an exceptional characteristic in the Chinese theory of cognition. The compound nature of knowledge and action is first evident in the meaning of the word "knowledge." The Chinese term points to both comprehension and "acceptance," and this so-called acceptance expresses a commitment to act in accordance with what is known and a judgment of either approval or disapproval. When students say they "know the meaning of participating in physical labor," this implies that they themselves are prepared to go and participate in physical labor.

Then again, this conflation of knowledge and action is expressed in the use of the term "meaning." When Chinese Marxists see conceptual knowledge and the meaning of knowing things mixed together, they are diverging from original Marxism. The meaning of knowing things usually implies comprehending a thing's value and importance to people, and can even point to the determination to act that comes according to the particular values implied in that meaning. On this point, the meaning assigned by the Chinese and the Western idea of "meaning" show clear differences. In contemporary Western philosophy, many philosophers influenced by spin-offs of the logical positivist school, make distinctions between cognitive and noncognitive meaning, or factual and emotive meaning. The meaning of knowledge rests only on whether the facts can reliably justify a belief to be true or false. The values conveyed express the speaker's feelings, and so are termed a narration of emotion.[21] In China there is no such division between the meaning of fact and emotion; when Chinese say they know the meaning of something, their factual, confirmable narration can include the preference of value judgment.

Finally, knowledge and action together are expressed in the use of the term "thought." This term has broad and narrow senses. In its narrow sense it concerns convictions about the material world and human society, or it is something a person uses to learn more about values in the world.

Chinese thought is different in that it often involves promptings to action, and because of this there is the saying, "Proletarian thought both scientifically knows the world and is a weapon to reconstruct the world." The broad meaning of thought points to psychological phenomena that are unrelated to the thought process and unrelated to knowledge about the world. This sense of "thought" can be translated as wish, attitude, or habit. In its narrow sense, thought and the cognitive factors of clustering have a clear partial overlap; in its broad sense, there is a similar overlap with emotional factors. From either approach thought often has the function of stimulating and directing actions.

In sum, in China knowledge can concern facts and also values; emotions and attached responses to value often accompany knowledge or convictions, and the motivation to act always urges a mode of action that is unified with the value produced in knowing the object. A special role of the state in China comes from the tendency to see close links between distinguishing objective facts, the attached value-judgment-generated emotions, and motivations to action, in addition to a conviction in human malleability. The state is recognized to have a responsibility to make sure that appropriate value judgments and correct motivations to action accompany people's knowledge of objective facts. And so the state has a basic responsibility to nurture people's "minds," and must take responsibility for people's thinking and the social environment.

Correspondingly, each individual's responsibility and free will are not nearly so important. This contrasts strikingly with the Western view. The theory of freedom and democracy holds that government should only concern itself with people's outer behavior and should not monitor people's thinking. Each person has his own free will, and so each should take full responsibility for his or her own self.

ZHU XI AND THE INTERNAL CONTRADICTIONS OF CONFUCIANISM

Compared to his two previous volumes, the third volume of the trilogy, *Images of Human Nature: A Sung Portrait*, presents an important development in Munro's research method. Where differences between the first and second volumes lie with the periodization of the history of thought between the early and modern periods, the third volume takes as its focus the period for which Zhu Xi can be studied as a representative figure. Beyond this, the third volume stresses the structural imagistic analogies that are especially important in Zhu Xi's system of thought, such as family, water, mirror, the body, plants, and the ruler. Munro shows that in the formation of Zhu Xi's philosophical system these images play a central role.

When analyzing Zhu Xi's thought, Munro reveals two sets of contradictions or tensions within the theoretical system of Confucianism. The first is between, on the one hand, the principle of family priority, and, on the other, the principle of universal love. Obviously, these polarities contain the possibility for conflict. In the pre-Qin period, the struggle between Confucians and Mohists had involved just this contradiction. The Mohists advocated unranked universal love, while the Confucians emphasized graded degrees of love, differentiating between kin and those outside kinship circles. Beyond this, the principle of treating kin as kin, giving them preferential consideration, and the principle of universal morality also was present as a contradiction. In the *Analects* Confucius opposes the son informing on his father, saying, "The father conceals the son, and the son conceals the father—the upright path lies in this."[22] But the *Zuozhuan* (Duke Zhao 14) quotes Confucius saying, "He did not hide anything involving his own kin ... he can be said to have been upright."[23] From this one can see that under certain circumstances, the principle of preferential treatment of kin, taking filiality as its core, can hardly avoid coming into conflict with the principle of a public ethic. And filiality will be an obstacle to the later Confucian advocacy of universal love among all living things. Reflecting this conflict, Zhu Xi criticized the Mohists, holding that they not only disparaged Nature's familial emotional bond, but also hoped to obliterate natural hierarchies in ethics.

Zhu Xi advocated the value principle of family preference, but also advocated realizing the altruistic principle of public spiritedness. But Zhu Xi did not succeed in resolving the relationship between these two. In particular he did not put forward actual methods of realizing altruism, so his successors by and large adhered to the principle of family preference. Because Zhu Xi's philosophy gradually became official orthodoxy, it perpetuated the tendency in Confucianism to weaken the idea of love of all things and humanism. In the end, this weakness in official Confucianism was criticized by the cultural enlightenment movements in the late Qing and early Republican period. Munro considers this to be a fundamental contradiction in Confucian philosophy.

Another contradiction in the Confucian theory of human nature is its stress on the cultivation of the self, placing the ethical self at one extreme, and, at the other, stress on obeying external ritual rules and authorities. Mencius believed in a heavenly endowed internal good nature and moral sense of right and wrong. Xunzi stressed external ritual rules and education. Between stressing either the exercise of individual autonomy, or external authority, the early Confucians failed to advocate a clear and operable principle of balance. Neither did Zhu Xi pay sufficient attention to or discuss these possible points of conflict. In Zhu Xi's argument, the self's manifestation of moral truth can unproblematically coexist with submission to various kinds of external authority. Between them there is no clear difference of priority or rank. Later Confucian thinkers and rulers, no matter which extreme they tended toward, have all been able to find justification in Zhu Xi's thought.

Against these weaknesses in Zhu Xi's thought, Munro holds that the conflict between family love and universal love does exist, but that both possibilities are contained in our inborn human nature. In recent years, Munro has again and again referred to evolutionary biology, to suggest that within the genes of the human species exists not only the seed of the selfish gene that gives priority to its own reproduction and therefore priority to the family members that share those genes, but also the seed of altruism beyond the family. He uses discoveries of experimental science in support of the traditional Confucian viewpoint, to put forth a new theory that resolves an internal contradiction in Confucian thought.

EVOLUTION OF THE IMPERIAL STYLE OF INQUIRY

The three books of Munro's trilogy pursue a common thread in discussing human nature. At the same time they lay out a Chinese method of thinking and its many-faceted influence. In his most recent work, *The Imperial Style of Inquiry in Twentieth Century China*, published in 1996, this topic is systematically summarized and further developed.

Although this book centers on the twentieth century, the "imperial style of inquiry" defined and discussed here is rooted in the time of Confucius and Mencius, develops through the Neo-Confucianism of the Song-Ming, and continues to have an impact in the twentieth century. This traditional Chinese inquiry, especially in the twentieth century, begins an interactive give-and-take with the objective style of knowledge cultivated in the modern West, gradually yielding to this modern mode of inquiry that has become synonymous with the scientific spirit. But as before, the imperial style of inquiry presents various positive and negative attributes.

So-called "inquiry" refers to the pursuit of what today is called knowledge and the methods of seeking it. But this description is far from sufficient. Inquiry also includes the quest for moral ideals, methods of moral education, and various methods and styles of resolving actual social problems. The concept of inquiry developed here arises out of the specific characteristics of Chinese philosophy; it eschews using Western philosophy's epistemological and knowledge concepts and their theoretical frame. Chinese thought systems and Western philosophy's division into systematic branches are clearly different. In China, in contrast to the West, the leading points in epistemology have always been clustered together, for example, the pursuit of morality, the cultivation of human nature, and the ordering of society. In Munro's second and third volumes he again and again points to and criticizes confusions of value and fact in Chinese traditional thought. In this book he focuses on the imperial style of inquiry to expand and deepen this investigation.

The imperial style of inquiry is interdependent with the traditional theory of the unity of heaven and humans, what Munro terms totalism. The belief that everything belongs to an interrelated order not only threads through the natural world, it also manifests itself in the human species. Later, this tradition became the mainstay of imperial power and the social hierarchy, and also conditioned and led to the traditional Confucian style of inquiry. Its main point is adherence to antecedent or traditional knowledge models or methods of solving problems, such as the well-field system of antiquity. It assigns the standard for knowledge and inquiry itself to external authorities, ultimately to the emperor. In the sphere of moral knowledge, Confucians believed that moral truth lies in the mind. So when seeking knowledge of external reality, one must be able to confirm it in light of the principles in the mind. But when these principles and external authorities came into conflict, the decision always went to political authority. The Confucian tradition also believed that the human mind, though not the *li* (principles), should change, and that rulers should act as spiritual teachers, taking on the role of moral authorities. In addition, the imperial style of inquiry has never clearly distinguished between facts and values—the "what is in fact" from the " what should be fact." Therefore, practitioners of traditional inquiry continue to take human value judgments and apply them to facts of objective existence, thereby distorting even scientific investigation and research.

In the twentieth century, China's imperial style of inquiry began to come in contact with the Western scientific method of knowing. This interaction was mutually disturbing, producing both conflict and fusion, with traditional inquiry gradually yielding its heretofore unchallenged position to epistemological principles that emphasize individual autonomy and pluralism, science, and objectivity. Philosophers, sociologists, scientists, and also political leaders all played important roles in this process. Especially interesting in this book is Munro's discussion of both how the thought of scholars such as Xiong Shili, He Lin, Liang Shuming, and Chen Lifu (also an official) is related to the imperial style of inquiry, and also the interaction of the thought and theories of political leaders such as Sun Yat-sen, Chiang Kai-shek (Jiang Jieshi), and Mao Zedong with traditional inquiry. Munro discusses how Mao successively established the Yan'an model, the Soviet model, and also the Daqing (an oil industry site) model, and gives concrete examples of how these models were implemented. The Yan'an model (pre-1949) established a union of the traditional and the new era's epistemological style. It emphasized investigation and study, stressed proceeding from actual conditions of China's rural war, and opposed book worship. This is a new tendency toward the development of an objective epistemological path. However, the Yan'an model also derived from the traditional approach in that political leaders wanted to unify the world, rectify people's minds, and transform the masses. This moral agenda seriously limited the ordinary person's epistemological agency. After 1949, Mao Zedong's Yan'an style of inquiry, with its emphasis on objectivity, was dropped. The traditional imperial mode, with its ideal of grand unity of the world, became paramount once again, supplemented by the influence of the Soviet-style inquiry. This shift brought calamitous consequences for China's development. By the 1980s, many of these were gradually being rectified. The scientific spirit advocated by progressive intellectuals in the first half of the twentieth century began to develop anew in the 1980s, and unofficially, a new stress on the agency of the individual in matters of inquiry began to emerge.

Although Munro strongly criticizes the various defects of the traditional style of inquiry, such as its mixing of fact and value, and the oppression of individual autonomy under political authority, at the same time he completely approves of the content of the traditional inquiry that is still meaningful in the present age. This content includes, for example, the harmony of man and nature, the acceptance of man's malleability, and the guiding function of model emulation. This analytical attitude is one we can usefully adopt in the current conflicts over old and new, and China and the West. At the same time, although he stresses the value of individual agency in the process of inquiry, his main point concerns methodology and utility; it is not about a total change of political system. He believes that indiscriminately copying Western values to change Chinese tradition is not possible.

LIFELONG SERVICE AND ONGOING CONTRIBUTIONS

The above is only a limited introduction to Professor Munro's major works. His other works have also made important contributions and remain influential. For example, his edited volume *Individualism and Holism: Studies in Confucian and Taoist Values* (1985) brings together the essays of important philosophers, historians, literary scholars, and sociologists such as Yu Yingshi, Ambrose King, Tu Weiming, A. C. Graham, Wm. Theodore de Bary, Chad Hansen, Irene Bloom, Arthur Danto, and Wolfgang Bauer. These authors not only constitute a cross-section of scholarship from the 1980s, they continue to be key figures in the study of Chinese thought and culture to the present day. Munro himself contributed an important article to this volume, as well as composing a lengthy introduction. Comparing Chinese and Western perspectives, he analyzed basic concepts relevant to the constructs of individualism and holism, such as uniqueness, privacy, autonomy, dignity, and so forth. He especially focused on Daoism because it was primarily the intellectuals of the Wei-Jin Neo-Daoist period who investigated and pursued uniqueness. The Confucian concept of the sage, in contrast, stresses the common nature of humans and ignores or suppresses individual autonomy and uniqueness. Modern Western thought, of course, emphasizes individuality, uniqueness, and autonomy and on this point has more in common with the Daoist tradition.

Since he began studying Chinese philosophy, Professor Munro has made a practice of immersing himself in and then borrowing insights from various fields and areas, including philosophy and sinology, early philology, education, psychology, and sociology. At the same time, he has over his career also pursued several profound questions such as: Why has Confucianism endured in China for two thousand years? He believes that this may be because certain aspects of Confucianism are in line with basic aspects of human nature. He has found new answers to this question in the discussions of seminars called "Culture and Cognition" and "Evolutionary Psychology," in which he recently participated. These groups periodically hold discussions that include perspectives from natural science, social science, and the humanities. What everyone is concerned about is the influence of culture on how people pursue knowledge and on the content of that knowledge, and the question as to how much of those pursuits is biological. In his cross-disciplinary investigations Munro has discovered that we can bring insights from new findings and theories in the natural sciences to bear in our analysis of traditional Chinese theories of human nature and ethics. His recent essays and lectures all derive from this approach. Some of these appear in the present volume.

Professor Munro not only strives to advance his own academic study and writing, he also devotes himself to teaching and guiding students. His many students, and their students in turn, are already teaching in universities, and some have become famous scholars. Many people, even those not his direct disciples, have received his help, guidance, and direction. The author of these remarks is among those who have benefited from his inclusive spirit of openness to all streams of thought and tireless teaching.

To promote the advancement of the study of Chinese philosophy and nurture those who study Chinese culture, Professor Munro has announced and taken the lead in contributing to the establishment of the Tang Junyi Fellowship in Chinese Philosophy at the University of Michigan. This may be the first fellowship named after a Chinese philosopher in the Western world. It is worth mentioning that Professor Munro is not alone in honoring Tang. The Philosophy Department of the Chinese University of Hong Kong has also established a Tang Junyi Lectureship. Munro has not only raised for us the quality of research in Chinese philosophy, he has also actively promoted the development of this subfield. This spirit, this effort, and this contribution are all worthy of our appreciation, study, and emulation.

Professor Munro has presented three lectures for the Ch'ien Mu (Qian Mu) Lectureship. The content of all three encompassed the two main topics of his long-term research: the concept of equality, including natural equality and equality of worth, and the question of individual autonomy. This has been at once a revealing instance of academic teaching-by-example and also an opportunity for us to taste a good academic brew. To extend our thanks and respect, let us attentively offer the couplet below to Professor Munro, who has made light of his trouble in coming to us from such a long distance.

Unveiling its intellectual grandeur, your work provides a meeting ground
for ancient and modern, Chinese and Western;
Revealing subtleties of scholarship, your insights inspire like a spring rain
nourishing Heaven and man, hearts and deeds.

The Ch'ien Mu Lectures

1

Lecture One:
Two Kinds of Equality

We who study ethics and seek its application in our unruly world today can, if we close our eyes for a moment, envision a truly equitable global society. This is a society in which the education systems assure equal opportunity to all children, and the content of education includes the contributions to ideas and technologies of peoples from the East and the West. It is also a society in which the worth of each individual is protected by the basic principles sanctioned by the United Nations, even when this means some lessening of the national sovereignty of individual countries. Here is the odyssey of thought about China and the United States by which I came to believe this vision is attainable.

In 1973, I co-led a delegation of educators to China. This was one of the first exchanges agreed upon during the 1972 Kissinger–Zhou Enlai talks in Shanghai. During my briefing of these educators, I explained that they were going to visit a society with a profound sense of hierarchy. It would be manifest in how our hosts behaved and in how their society was organized. Most of the delegation chastised me for ignoring the dramatic news they had read in the papers: China had abolished ranks in the military and in some other services. No more insignias separating officers from enlisted soldiers. So when we crossed the border into China at Luohu my fellow delegates were surprised at our Chinese host asking me for our protocol list immediately after greeting us. This list indicated our members' respective ranks in the group. The Chinese wanted the list so they would know who were the group's leaders, so their leaders could inform ours of daily plans. They wanted to know who should sit in the Red Flag limousine and who would ride in the grey bus. We had entered a society that at that time prized social equality, yet also practiced institutionalized social inequality.

In premodern China, every Confucian knew the Mencian tenets that "Everyman can be a Yao or a Shun," and "The sage and I are the same in kind." These assertions seem close in spirit to the American founding principle that "All men are created equal." And yet, at the same time, premodern China was also known for its view that, just as Heaven is high and the earth low, so the distinction of superior and inferior is necessary in human society. The emperor is at the top, the grades of civil servants or scholar-officials come next, and on down the social role ladder. The claim that everyman can be a sage was never developed in the early period into a doctrine of the equal worth of all persons, based on that potentiality. For adults, degrees of worth were the rule.

We live in an era in which most developed societies assume that equality is a positive value for creating the good society. This is revealed in the Preamble to the U.N.'s *Universal Declaration of Human Rights*, which refers to the equal and inalienable rights of all members of the human family as the foundation of freedom, justice, and peace. The presumption means that there must be very clear reasons for treating some people differently, in the degrees of respect and rights we accord them. We usually do not have to justify treating people the same. But what is this thing called "equality"? Answering this question will provide us a new tool for understanding important aspects of Chinese culture, past, present, and future, and what that culture shares or does not share with the West. Our process involves distinguishing between the different meanings of equality and how they rank in importance in China and the West across time. I will talk first about natural equality, then about equality of worth, and finally about equal treatment of all people by their societies.

NATURAL EQUALITY

"Natural equality" is a descriptive term that we use today, not a term used by early Chinese.[1] It refers to the common attributes or characteristics with which all people are born. But it accurately covers the Mencian position that all people are born with "the four minds": compassion, shame, respect, and right/wrong; exercising these four is the path to sagehood. It says nothing about all people having exactly identical potential to be a sage. It is compatible with the *Analects* 16.9 statement that some people are born knowing, which puts them on a higher plane from others. Obviously some people are tall and others short. So the

Mencian position implies a value judgment about what is the most important of the human traits, and those are the ones that are equally possessed. Compassion is the most important trait, the essential human quality, which is manifest as humaneness (*ren*). It emerges in the relation between caregiver and child, then extends to other kin, and can and should be extended beyond the family. This extension of caring beyond the nuclear family is what we call altruism. Starting in the Zhou period, writers described it as reciprocal. They said, "There is no kindness (*de*) that is not requited."[2] The ruler who treats the people with kindness receives in return their affection and future loyal service. Parentlike officials (*fumu guan*) who provide educational and economic nurturance to the people receive in exchange their transformed characters and obedience, leading to social harmony. Mencius's idea of the mind of right and wrong refers to an evaluative mind that both knows what is right and wrong and also commands the person to act accordingly. It is close to an aspect of what people in the West call an innate moral sense. The Mencian position on all of these matters was accepted and reinforced by Zhu Xi (1130–1200) of the Southern Song. Through the use of his writings in the school curriculum and in the preparation for civil service examinations after 1313, these ideas achieved a certain orthodoxy and wide acceptance.

Natural equality is close to but different in emphasis from equality of worth or value that became important in the West after the Reformation. Natural equality stresses primarily the description of common inborn traits. Secondarily, it may have implications for how people should be treated in terms of food and education. In contrast, the emphasis in evaluative equality in the West is on equal worth first and foremost as a justification for equal treatment before the law. It requires protections for individuals against their rulers or against groups by referring to the individual's rights. It is based in the Western belief that God loves all souls equally, having created them in His image.

Natural equality often deals with factual matters about humans that leaders will observe if they wish to be effective. It tells rulers what kind of policies will and will not work, by virtue of their compatibility with the human condition. Ensuring that people have food and education to develop their traits are such policies, in Confucian thought. The concept of natural equality also implies that all people, including rulers, need to be mindful of their own inborn natures, in order properly to cultivate themselves. Why is natural equality important in the study of Chinese culture? One reason is because it helps us to understand how Confucians were able to accommodate both a belief in natural social hierarchies and also the egalitarian belief that anyone can be a sage. The Confucian approach stems directly from the attribution of the same essential traits to all humans at birth. It led to one of China's great contributions to world political organizations, the civil service examination system. "Merit" has been the criterion that harmonizes natural equality with hierarchy, by assigning political and economic privilege to those among the people who make the effort to improve themselves through education. In traditional China, this development was measured in terms of literacy and character refinement. Those who developed themselves, with the state's aid, were counted meritorious.

In reality, there were always exceptions to the merit principle in selecting people for positions of privilege: bias against women eliminated half the population from competition at the start; some elite members of officialdom procured rank for their offspring without their having to take the exams; children of prostitutes and canal boatmen were sometimes prohibited from taking the examinations; and ethnic bias favored different groups at different times, for instance, Mongols during the Yuan period. Still, education was considered to be the solution to urgent political and social problems, right through the twentieth century. Its prominence reflects an optimistic assessment of people's egalitarian potential.

The idea of natural equality also helped shape other belief systems in China. Among the distinctively Chinese schools of Buddhism, Tiantai and Chan both assert that the Buddha nature is equally present in all people. This refers to the so-called "pure mind," different from our ordinary mind, which is subject to errors of perception and judgment. Through the pure mind, each individual can attain Buddhahood. In India this doctrine was hotly debated, but the emphasis was on those few people who are able to spend their lives in ascetic meditation and thereby can attain that highest state. The idea of equal possession of the Buddha nature was also debated for some time in China, but in the end it prevailed. The Mencian idea that anyone can be a sage seems to have laid the foundation for this later doctrine.

But the idea of natural equality is important not only for what it contributed to Chinese culture in the past, but also for what it can contribute today to international discussions of ethics. As we will see, the Chinese view of natural equality meshes in significant ways with emerging developments in Western ethics. A major trend in ethics has developed from findings of the new biology, beginning with the 1950s discoveries in genetics by Watson and Crick. The disciplines most involved in generating the new information are evolutionary biology and evolutionary psychology. Evolutionary biology is the attempt to link social (not only human) behavior to evolutionary theory about the survival of the fittest. Its evolutionary interest is in the struggles of genes to maximize their own reproduction, generation after generation. In this connection, evolutionary biology studies the influences of genes on behavioral traits such as kinship relations. It also accepts the mutual interaction of genes and culture. Evolutionary psychology focuses on how the architecture of the mind evolved over time. That means it is concerned with the rules hardwired in the brain that account for such things as language acquisition and kinship relations. Among others, the works of Edward O. Wilson, a Harvard biologist, and Steven Pinker, a psychologist, helped shape these trends. Both of these scientists write about a "common human nature," a concept that some of their colleagues in philosophy, anthropology, and biology go so far as to deny has any meaning at all. These developments in evolutionary biology and psychology intersect with strong traditions in Chinese Confucian culture. This is why I focus on them right now. I have become especially conscious of them by participating in a couple of faculty seminars at the University of Michigan with psychologists, psychiatrists, and even primatologists. What I find intriguing about the works of Wilson, Pinker, and other evolutionary scientists is that they converge with the Mencian principles that have endured so long in China.

Three of these convergences appear in the following citations. The writers refer, in sequence, to the primacy of family ties (first in our consciousness and priorities), to the existence of a universal moral sense based, in part, on sympathy, and finally to people's predisposition to share and, given sufficient information, to cooperate, based on a system of reciprocal altruism.

> Among the traits with documented heritability, those closest to moral aptitude are empathy to the distress of others and certain processes of attachment between infants and their caregivers. To the heritability of moral aptitude add the abundant evidence of history that cooperative individuals generally survive longer and leave more offspring. It is to be expected that in the course of evolutionary history, genes predisposing people toward cooperative behavior would have come to predominate in the human population as a whole. Such a process, repeated through thousands of generations inevitably gave birth to the moral sentiments. With the exception

of stone psychopaths (if any truly exist), these instincts are vividly experienced by every person variously as conscience, self-respect, remorse, empathy, humility, and moral outrage.[3]

Lastly, regarding reciprocal altruism, one writer describes it this way,

> A gene that repaid kindness with kindness could thus have spread through the extended family, and, by interbreeding, to other families, where it would thrive on the same logic.[4]

Empirical research has included the study of warning calls made by birds, fish, dolphins, primates, bats, and impalas. The calls put the caller in danger by revealing its own location. But surviving animals or birds or fish repay the altruism of the call-giver, whose kind may be saved by the future calls of the survivors.[5]

It may be useful for us to reinforce the early Confucian and the biological ideas that kindness is often reciprocated. The findings of modern game theory confirm the value of kindness, sharing, or cooperation beyond the family, when information about common interests is also shared. Game theory results reveal that cooperation may benefit social outcomes in the long run, and this dovetails nicely with biological findings about reciprocal altruism.

Aside from its resonance with recent thinking about genetically predispositioned cooperation and reciprocity, the Mencian legacy of a naturally equal human nature is important for world culture today because many of its claims are based on accurate descriptions of human social life. Only those social policies that are consistent with the way human beings really live, have a reasonable chance of long term success. In contrast, one of the most popular Western ethical stances—utilitarianism—in fact, includes a profoundly alienating aspect, because it runs contrary to the way people live. People will act in accordance with rules they find emotionally compelling, and one aspect of utilitarianism falls fatally short in this regard.

I can accept the utilitarian idea that right and wrong are in part a function of the pain/happiness consequences of acts, and that each person is the best judge of his or her interests, where happiness is concerned. With Mill, I accept the nuance that education can improve the judgment of some people. But Bentham, J. S. Mill, and the present day utilitarian Peter Singer also affirm a point that I cannot accept, and I suspect others feel the same.[6] This is that in calculating the cost/benefit consequences of deeds, "each [person is] to count for one and none for more than one."

This produces an equality of right, of equal rightful claims to a voice in the allocation of resources by each person. I must reject the view that, when I am the agent, all other people share an equal right or claim on my concerns. Any ethics such as utilitarianism that tells me to ignore the preferential affection I have for my close kin and neighbors has a good chance of alienating me. It may cause me to ignore it. It is not useful as a tenet of ethics. I legitimately treat each of my kin as counting for *more* than other individuals in the allocation of my resources and caring.

If anyone is looking for evidence of the utilitarian error here, he need only look at the last few lines of a profile of Peter Singer in *The New Yorker* magazine. Tragically, his mother fell ill with Alzheimer's disease, and he chose to spend a great deal of money on her private care beyond what would be provided by the utilitarian "equal claim on resources by all individuals," or, be provided by public facilities. When asked how he squared this with his position that we should do what is morally right without regard for family relations, he replied, "Perhaps it is more difficult than I thought before, because it is different when it's your mother."[7]

I believe that the best way to reply to the utilitarian on this matter is to focus on the Mencian ideas that have been reasserted by evolutionary biology. Those ideas easily accommodate the choice that Singer eventually made. Preferential treatment for kin is justified on the basis of our natural emotional bonds to them. But this is not the end of concern for non-kin, to which I will turn in a moment. The laws to which I will then refer can help set limits on that preferential treatment of kin.

Let us consider an objection to this approach. For some people, to hear the word "biological" in this context is to hear a warning. That warning alerts them to any theory that affirms genetic determinism by tracing all human actions to biological causes over which the individual has no control. But I make no reductionist claim. I believe that people do exhibit common behavioral tendencies. The Confucian position focuses on those tendencies, one of which is to act in accordance with sympathy and in cooperation, both with kin and with out-groups. This inborn disposition, however, is in practice compatible with free will, where free will means the individual's capacity also to make choices not determined by his genes or by neighbors or any coercive cause. Those choices may in fact involve acting contrary to a tendency that is biologically favored. For example, the psychologist Steven Pinker used the example of the individual deciding against having children.[8]

Just because you know your own tendencies does not mean you are locked into submitting to them. Instead, to be free *and* responsible is to know your tendencies, so as to be alert and able to control or guide them. This is to know yourself. Some people draw strange conclusions from biological research. A recent example involves the study published about male primates engaging in gang rape (*A Natural History of Rape: Biological Bases of Sexual Coercion*).[9] This book caused a furor in the United States. Its authors, Randy Thornhill, an evolutionary biologist, and Craig T. Palmer, an evolutionary anthropologist, state, "… there is no doubt that rape has evolutionary—and thus genetic—origins." Those who attacked the authors argued that they were trying to justify sexually predatory behavior in human males. Better to ask whether all men have sexually predatory tendencies. If so, men might learn which behavioral tendencies they need to control. So the fact that *tendencies* may have a genetic basis does not mean they determine or justify behavior by an individual.

EQUALITY OF WORTH

Equality of worth is a judgmental or evaluative concept, which carries the suggestion that all people should be treated alike, unless good reasons are given. The worth in question is intrinsic value, not as simply a means to some other goal, and it applies to every individual. It is independent of actual rank, skill, or power. The emphasis in the West has been on treating people as equal before the law, respecting their individual rights against the whims of rulers or groups. Thomas Jefferson was especially interested in laws that ensure equal opportunity of education, which he sought in Virginia. It is embodied in the 14th Amendment to the U.S. Constitution. It requires that people we do not know have equal protection under the law. It requires that, when in need, they become the recipients of help from local or global aid organizations. Equality of worth claims that, from a certain perspective, all people have some shared basic worth. Great differences exist among commentators as to where the basis or source of that worth lies, as I will show. The chief contenders, on the one hand, are some of those influenced by the new evolutionary sciences, and, on the other, those who trace the source to God or to a heavenly way (*tiandao*). This issue of equal protection has been a matter of considerable practical consequence at my own university. Plaintiffs sued the University of Michigan in the U.S. Supreme Court on the charge that the

University's admission's policies in its undergraduate college and Law School have violated the equal protection principle. That under-graduate policy had given extra admission points to "underrepresented minorities."

The concept of equal worth is important to world culture, for example, because those who practice racial discrimination have generally justified their brutal treatment of out groups by claiming that the members of out groups are less than human. In fact, the brutal treatment has involved claims about both natural inequality and inequality of worth. This was done by the Nazis in Germany, by slaveholders in the United States and Latin America up to the nineteenth century, and by white settlers in Australia. These people were concerned with affirming *unequal* worth as well as the absence of certain natural traits like reasoning ability or a sense of homelands. They were not concerned with trying to understand what human nature really is. They justified their claims of inequality by reference to popular cliches or pseudo science or power relations.

I will give one example, borrowed from the Australian philosopher Raimond Gaita.[10] White settlers in Australia would not accept that aborigines had a special relation to their land or were capable of regarding it as their "own native place." So the settlers declared the land empty and took it. Neither could they believe that the aborigines had properly parental relations to their own children. So they took their lands and they also took children of mixed blood, who were put in institutions or foster homes. Not until 1992 did the High Court in Australia send down a judgment, known as Mabo, giving back to aborigines title to their native lands. On September 29, 2002, a federal judge in Australia returned formal control of a chunk of northwest Australia bigger than Greece to the Martu people. In 1997 parliament revoked the former policy on mixed blood children after studying a report on those children entitled, *Bringing Them Home*.

Westerners had minimal interest in equality or equality of worth until the modern era, beginning in the sixteenth century. Before then, many were influenced by the Platonic legacy, spelled out in the *Republic*, which outlined natural gradations in both the structure and the worth of souls. One had either a gold, silver, or brass soul, paralleling the hierarchy of reason, high spirit/motivation, and physical desires. If Plato's plan for selective breeding were followed, Platonists believed, those with gold souls would usually perpetuate themselves. Aristotle believed that most people are slaves by nature. His positions also assumed a natural inequality of reasoning ability. These differences from birth through adulthood justified claims of inequality of worth, and therefore of status and of political authority. So a dominant belief in inequalities of ability and worth was used to justify a "natural" aristocracy. This remained the dominant philosophical claim until the French philosopher Descartes took the position that "the power of judging well and of distinguishing between the true and the false, which, properly speaking, is what is called good sense, or reason, is by nature equal in all men." And the Reformation in the beginning of the sixteenth century saw the principle of equal worth affirmed on the argument that all people are the objects of God's love and have souls in His image. This train of thinking eventually gave rise to the American founders claim that "all men are created equal." They believed that equality can be achieved in fact through laws that protect equally possessed rights.

Much earlier than in the West, Neo-Confucian thinkers of the Song dynasty (960–1279) had developed an explicit case for the equal worth of persons, *from a certain perspective* (but not every perspective). This formulation does not go far enough, but it does contain the basis from which to generate an emotionally charged view of all individuals as worthy of love, attention, and respect based on the heavenly origin of their innate ability to know moral principles.

This notion of equal worth coexisted with an older tradition that supported fixed social roles exemplified by those in the family. The hierarchical family analogy was used to justify insistence that people remain in their assigned social positions. These relationships involve authority and obedience, and are supposedly modeled on nature.

But to turn from hierarchy to equality, we find again the coexistence of seeming contradictions. In their discussions of equal worth, Song thinkers relied on a pre-Song image or analogy used by several schools for the common heavenly nature found in all humans. Because heaven endows the people's natures, rulers should nurture them. That image is pure or clear water, and the heavenly nature it refers to supplies the universal energy and pattern according to which humans develop over time. What is equal about people is manifested in the natural equality we found in Mencius, namely the ethico-biological traits: a preference for kinship love, reciprocal altruism, and a moral sense whose content is shame and a conscience about right and wrong. However, in the Song, what is new is that there is a well developed theory about a transcendental origin for these traits, in the heavenly principles (*tianli*) or heavenly way (*tiandao*). To the already existing idea of natural equality, this adds a new source of worth: the heavenly principles or heavenly way.This theory is a vast enlargement from the single reference in the Mencius to a link between heaven and human nature.[11] Here is Zhu Xi's explanation:

> The clear water represents the goodness of the nature…. However, although a person is muddied by his material endowment and so flows into doing evil, it is never the case that his nature is not there with him… Therefore, because of this, "men should not fail to exert the effort to purify themselves." Only if a person is able through study to overcome the material endowment will he know that the nature is vast and never decayed, and is the "original water."[12]

Here the common principle of humanity imagined as pure or clear water from a spring source (the heavenly way/*tiandao*) that flows through and interpenetrates all things explains the potential equal worth of all living things by claiming they have a common source. The image generates both reverence for the original pure source and some knowledge of and feeling of unity with all that is linked by the flow. This natural potential for cognition and moral emotion become the basis for a kind of equality of worth in all people. It is pure and clear, not dirty and muddy. The varying quality of actual individual natures is a function of their material endowment or physical nature, which the pure principle encounters. The picture of water sullied by dirt is intended also to motivate the person to purify what material nature has sullied. Each person's original nature is equally worthy and constitutes the basis for individual improvement, if one accepts the premise about the heavenly origin of the nature. This then would reinforce the ruler's and officials' obligation to provide economic livelihood and education. People would be deserving objects of consideration because they can recover the mind that has transcendental worth. So efforts to develop oneself and teach others follow from this analogy of Zhu Xi.

Zhu Xi, as champion of this principle, played a direct role in the growth of education that began in the Song. Although the 1044 edict requiring a state-sponsored school in each prefecture, and other events, predate his efforts in the spread of education, Zhu still had a significant role in developing the versions of texts and commentaries that would be widely used as curricula in the national and private schools.

Thus, there is plenty of evidence that within Chinese culture lie powerful claims about what we today call both natural equality and equality of worth. At the same time the widespread practice of equal treatment has not emerged. For one thing, the concurrent belief in the naturalness of social hierarchies and the prominence of the hierarchical family as the model for all social organizations also persists.

Expanding educational opportunity is one way for the elite to show belief in equal worth. Of course, in imperial China it was also a way to indoctrinate the population so as to achieve order, and it was a way to produce a pool of potential civil officials. Some steps were taken to extend education to the poor and rural folk during the imperial period. One was the establishment of unofficial schools, the curriculum of which was patterned after that in the official schools. "Charity schools" (*yixue*) at the primary level might be financed by a clan or group of gentry; community schools (*shexue*) financed by local magistrates sprang up beginning in the early Ming, as did private academies (*shuyuan*). Another measure to educate local commoners involved informal educa- tion. As early as the Han, Confucian sermons were delivered to illiterates by village elders. Periodic market town lectures for mutual moral reinforcement were revived by the Shunzhi emperor of the Qing (1644– 1661).[13] Still, the percentage of the population benefitting from these approaches was small and the effectiveness of the informal measures unclear.

So where do solutions lie in our present day world, for correcting the split between egalitarian ideal about equal worth and social practice? I believe they will emerge from how we deal with the contradiction between, on the one hand, justifiable preferential affection for kin, and on the other, belief in the equal worth of all people. The kin preference is part of our nature and cannot be ignored. At the same time, while retaining the belief in the equal worth of all persons, we must revise its formulation by Zhu Xi, so as to shift its basis from *tiandao* to biology. To deal with the contradiction requires enriching the idea of equal worth beyond what Song-Ming Confucians had proposed.

The equal worth idea still needs to have its content expanded. To do this I will present my own value standard. It is twofold. One part, to which I have already referred is utilitarian, in that it treats absence of suffering and presence of joy as giving content to right and good (though it rejects the point criticized above about an equality of right to my resources). The other part is a commitment to equality of human worth based on shared human traits. These certainly include the traits of concern to the first part of the standard: the ability to feel joy and suffering. But it adds the additional trait of love, as a major source of joy and as something that almost all humans have experienced and recognize receiving or giving.

In believing like Raimond Gaita that part of the basis of worth is being the object of love, I am not referring to the religious idea of God's love.[14] I refer to two dimensions of love. One is the now familiar biological love of child for parent or of parent for child. It is part of our common humanity and our ability to become good people by expanding the scope of that love at least to our extended family and some of our community. But by itself that initial love is transitory and limited. Equal worth cannot come simply from that root kinship love. In addition, a second fact must be tied to it: almost everyone is or has been the recipient of another person's love and kindness, and wants that type of love. As social animals, we find in it one source of self-worth, for which humans also have an innate desire. Most people have been the object of love, initially from our parents or caregivers, later from both of them, and then from an expanding circle of people beyond them. Although our own love may not extend to those outside our networks, we must recognize that other people are also the objects of *someone's* love. This is true regardless of gender or race. I consider this as a Chinese gift to ethics because Mencius was one of the first who advocated that people "Treat with the reverence due to age the elders in your own family, so that the elders in the families of others shall be similarly treated; treat with the kindness due to youth the young in your own family, so that the young in the families of others shall be similarly treated."[15] Mozi would have agreed with Mencius, having said something similar, but Mozi would not have accepted the parallel Confucian preferential love for kin. Unfortunately, Confucians did not go on to develop in detail the idea that, to have been the target of someone's love, bestows worth on all humans.

A final basis for enriching the idea of equal worth lies in the Western idea of autonomy. The Protestant Reformation provided the idea of the private individual conscience, independent of church or civil hierarchy. Kant contributed the idea that each person is free and worthy of respect because he or she has the ability to know moral principles through reason and can apply them to his or her own thinking and behavior. Autonomy is central to the European view of what a person is. Psychologists now treat it as something for which humans have an innate desire.[16] But, autonomy must be officially encouraged in order to be used. This was noted in 1848 by Alexis de Tocqueville, the great French commentator on the United States, after his travels there. He was concerned that, with the achievement of social *equality*, there is a great danger that the ideas of individuals would be dominated by majority public opinion. He wrote:

> Thus it might happen that, having broken down all the bonds which classes or men formerly imposed on it, the human spirit might bind itself in tight fetters to the general will of the greatest number.[17]

Autonomy exists when a person's actions, including both conduct and deliberations, are the result of his own choice rather than of the restraining threats or causes from some other individual or group. The value of the individual person's autonomy to society comes from our encouraging its use because of its practical benefit to all of us. Thus I regard it as the third ingredient of human worth. With autonomy comes responsibility for acts, and responsibility is needed as a deterrence to socially harmful conduct.[18] This linkage of choice and individual responsibility has not been historically as strong in China as in the West. One reason is that in the West the linkage was a necessary part of the Church's attempt to free an omnipotent God from responsibility for evil by tying evil to bad choices by individuals. The individuals then suffer the consequences. Many of the early Chinese texts indicate that good or bad consequences of good or bad deeds occur generations later as good or bad fortune for the extended family. They do not necessarily occur to the individual making choices, as in the West.

The other reason that autonomy is a source of worth is that autonomy, as opposed to obeying the conventions of popular opinion, has con-siderable instrumental value. It promotes good problem solving. With autonomy, individuals feel free and motivated to put forth their own hypotheses when they study a social or any other type of problem. Autonomy is a necessary condition for variability in proposed solutions. Among various competing theories, some will prevail, due to broad recognition of their explanatory strength, breadth of application, and problem-solving ability. This approach opposes single models and single authorities, such as those presented by political figures with an agenda defined by narrow interests or community officials who wish to create uniform public opinion. It does not oppose the authority of peers. There is a place for peer evaluation and correction. So, like nurturance, the encouragement of autonomy must be guaranteed by laws governing belief, speech, and the dissemination of ideas.

Now to the conflict between the idea of equal worth and that of graded or unequal love. The idea of equal worth applies only when the topic is the perspective of the recipients of actions and of any third party judge or observer of them. They know that normally everyone avoids suffering or seeks joy, and has been the target of someone's love. Normally, all persons are somewhat aware of these feelings and where they come from. This gives the objective judges (any citizen) a duty, on behalf of society, to recognize equality of worth by supporting the protection of people through law, national and international. Here is where the topic of "human rights" is relevant.

From the perspective of the actor or person who loves, however, the worth of the target of his love varies. From his point of view, people are of unequal worth. Worth is graded, depending of the degree of love bestowed, usually a function of the kind of relationship involved, especially those involving kin. This results in unequal distribution of the individual's resources that can affect the recipient's joy and suffering. So there is a public or legal place for equal worth and a private sphere for unequal worth. There is no alternative to a life constantly balancing these often conflicting claims.

Some Westerners may anchor their ethics in beliefs about a divine design in the universe or the commands of God, consistent with the Christian tradition, rather than in biology. Similarly, some Confucians may anchor their ethical principles in beliefs about a heavenly way (*tiandao*) or in the belief that human nature comes from Heaven. This is certainly consistent with the Confucian tradition. These beliefs have psychological and aesthetic benefits. They encourage us ecologically to prize the natural world of plants, animals, and resources in which we live, as well as to prize its people. I have no objection to people taking this position. But consider again the citations I gave from Wilson and others about the moral sentiments, empathy, cooperation, and reciprocal altruism. They show that there are intersections between the new biology and ethics. Biology intersects with the idea in Mencian ethics of natural equality, not with the Zhu Xi idea of a pure heavenly source for our natures. So I would urge Chinese ethicists who wish to join the international discourse on values to focus on our common biological nature. The Confucian Heaven is not likely to be understood clearly or be engaging by the international audience. At the same time, I would recommend that Westerners switch from anchoring their idea of equal worth in the notion that God loves all souls equally, to, instead anchoring it, among other places, in a biological basis, namely a universal, expandable, kinship love.

How to ensure that a wide scope of persons is given legal protections and caring treatment? One possible answer lies with the Mencian power of example, making those who do act altruistically the model for others. The second lies with the power of empathy for people we do not know. This can be fostered by literature and the honest portrayal of others in the arts. Professor Tang Junyi has written eloquently about empathic responses (*ganying* and *gandong*), and the changes that they cause in the person feeling them. Like most Chinese ethicists, he was acutely aware of the motivating energy of the emotions. This is one reason why the images of civil war victims in the former Yugoslavia and in Rawanda have been so influential. Finally, I believe we provide the ultimate safety net for others by supporting laws and institutions that protect and provide for them in ways that we as individuals cannot.

One of the main institutional ways in which we ensure that all people are accorded love and nurturance on the basis of their worth is through education. This is manifest in contemporary China in the establishment of rural schools and rural teachers colleges, whose graduates return to the villages to teach. There have been economic obstacles to doing this. Poor areas have fewer resources to pay for the physical facilities and supplies, poor families have less money for school fees, and, since daughters marry outside the family, there is less incentive to invest in educating them. Nevertheless, astounding progress has been made since the 1949, when the population that was 80 percent illiterate. By 1980 adult literacy had reached 70 percent, and most children received a primary education. This success must then be due in some measure to promoting "equal treatment," based on equal worth, in the form of equal opportunity. That goal was initially applied to school access and has now shifted to school quality. The 1995 Education Law states that all citizens will have equal opportunity for a quality education, and in 1999 the State Council decreed that this especially applied to poor and Western minority regions.[19] But there remains a substantial rural-urban gap because of the economic obstacles. This is especially evident at the college entry level, where rural students are underrepresented. So, as of this writing, equal opportunity in the rural areas remains a pious hope, not a fact. Equal opportunity has been defined this way:

> Man ... has equality of opportunity with others when he is free to choose any occupation he is fit for, and when the means of acquiring that fitness is limited only be defects of nature or morals, and not by lack of education or wealth or social prestige.[20]

Education helps implement the equality of opportunity by which we manifest our belief in equal worth.

In the final analysis, the stability of the value of equal worth depends on an individual's emotional commitment to it. As Randolph M. Nesse has written, "The emotional capacity for commitment seems to be a human universal."[21] Commitments generate trust in other people. Trust leads to predictability and therefore to social order. Those who make the commitments to equal worth, even at a cost to themselves or their kin, may positively influence others. They gain for themselves the same legal protections they support for others, but do not in additional ways gain the reciprocal benefits that flow from altruism.

Equality of worth has rich content, indeed, when it involves these shared human traits: their awareness of joy and suffering, their innate and expandable kinship love, coupled with their being the object of someone else's love or sympathy, and their awareness of their own autonomy. In this sense, equality of worth is compatible with hierarchies of social status that stem from unequal wealth or power. It is compatible with limousines and buses. It coexists with my own preferential treatment of my own family members and neighbors. But having wealth and power do *not* provide good reasons for unequal or special treatment before the law. Together, the traits making up the content of equal worth do argue for equal legal protection, including educational opportunities. This rich conceptual form of equal worth owes much to Chinese culture, some to modern biology, and some to the Western value of individual autonomy. In other words, it owes much to the new communication across cultures and academic disciplines. In the end, these exchanges benefit us all. They teach us how to implement the educational and legal means by which we can manifest our commitment to the value of equal worth and to the acknowledgement of our common human nature.

2

Lecture Two:
Two Objects of Our Affection:
What We Can Learn from Zhu Xi

How do we think? The part of the answer on which I focus reveals an inseparable linkage of cognition (knowing and thinking) and the emotions. This is an overriding theme of this essay. As examples, I will use the emotions of sympathy and fear. The mode of thought with which I am concerned is images or pictorial analogies used to explain theoretical positions.

This linkage appears in textual writings from the Southern Song. We today are only about fifty generations removed from Zhu Xi. Changes in gene structures between people than and people now would be too small to affect how we think. In the absence of exhaustive controlled studies by current scientists, there is a strong argument for making use of the voluminous written record bearing on the topic from earlier generations in a search for evidence. Recent studies by neurologists, such as Antonio Damasio, confirm the ties of cognition and the emotions. Among other things, the emotions motivate action in accordance with thought.

These ties may be purposively made. This is a practice Zhu Xi insisted we should observe when he discussed how epistemology and ethics go together. He had in mind that our efforts to know objects generally should be combined with having sympathy for them. Otherwise, the knowledge is incomplete. Or, the intertwining of emotion and cognition may be socially impressed on persons. I cite examples of how fear affected the value priorities of some of Zhu Xi's contemporaries, changing the priorities from those they had learned from teachers and even accepted in principle. In our own historical era, American presidents have made military and political decisions contrary to the conclusions of reasoning based on all available empirical evidence. Vietnam is an example of a situation in which fear of being considered weak or the person who "lost the war" trumped those rational conclusions favoring concluding the country's involvement in the war.

In addition to the overriding theme about how we think, I have a specific topic. It is an enduring matter. Whether the topic is Zhu Xi in the twelfth century, or us today, a key ethical questions remains the same. How can people resolve the competing claims of preferential affection for family and neighbors with the altruistic caring for others? If the former is justified by our biological constitution, the latter seems implied by the idea of some degree of equal worth among all humans. In this paper I both analyze Zhu Xi's approach and evaluate it.

My method is the study of the pictorial images used by Zhu Xi to explain his theories. Those images perform two functions, structural and emotive. An image structures the relations between disparate facts to which a theory applies, calling attention to certain aspects of the relationship. For example, the plant or tree image suggests the image of successive stages (as in stages of growth). And, because of the image's familiarity within the culture, it also elicits an emotional response to those facts, thereby uncovering a value that Zhu Xi wishes to affirm. So the method deals with how people think, namely sometimes pictorially. And this uncovers the linkage of thinking and the emotions.

The means offered by Zhu to harmonize the competing claims of family and other living things are both epistemological and ethical. He uses the images of the light source (mirror, lamp) and of the body in working out the part of his reply that concerns how the individual should behave. Successful resolution of the conflict is a condition he calls attaining "impartiality" (*gong*). This is the sage-like knowledge of and affection for a wide range of persons and creatures beyond the family boundaries. It is a union of the subjective and objective. Later I will introduce two other images, the plant and the gardener, that explain his theory of how the process to impartiality is part of a natural process of change.[1]

In taking the effort to deal with these matters, Zhu's immediate goal was to make a reply to the Buddhists, who he perceived as advocating escape, withdrawal, or retirement from family and from the world. He identified the root of their error to lie in treating the mind as empty, rather than as innately predisposed to identify with and enter into relations with people and things. Instead of being empty, according to Zhu, mind contains the principles (*li*) of all things. This refers to what accounts for the orderly changes that things can and should undergo. So mind and things are related through the sharing of principles (*li*). His idea is much the same as that found in Western thinkers from Plato to Kepler, who believed that the mathematical structure of the world has a counterpart in the minds of people. For Zhu, the objects of knowledge or study can be either concrete things (a bamboo plant), a relationship (father-son), or an idea in a text.

THE LAMP AND THE BODY

The image of light provides the structure that makes the concept of subjective-objective union intelligible. The individual first closes the gap between himself and an increasingly broad range of other living things by getting to know them. This is explained as light projected from a source that establishes verifiable contact between source and object, in this case self and others. Within the mind, principles are self-bright and capable of illuminating their objective counterparts. In the West, both Augustine and Descartes spoke of reason as like a natural light of the mind, and the innate ideas are God's self-bright gift to it. In China, the mirror image provides an additional factor, required by Zhu Xi's portrayal of knowledge acquisition as a round trip by the light. The light goes from the mirror light source to the object, from which it is reflected back to the mirror mind, brightening and clarifying the image already there in the mind. The term *zhao* refers to the mirror's capacity to illuminate and to reflect back. Mind and things can remain different, yet the mind is capable of contacting the object, thereby gaining direct knowledge of it.

Zhu described the attainment of impartiality and comprehensive knowledge by pointing to a candle. He said that if a candle is placed in the middle of a room, it illuminates everything in the room and there is no place for something bad to hide. When knowledge has not been completely extended, it is as though the candle (lamp) has a shade over it. One sees as far as the light reaches, but where the light does not reach, all is dark. Anything evil that may lie beyond the reach of the light cannot be seen. He pointed to a candle and said:

> It is like lighting a wax candle in the middle [of the room]. The light penetrates so that no spot is left unilluminated. Although one wishes to bring a bad thing in, there is no place to put it [where it cannot be detected]. Naturally there is no place for it. When knowledge is not completed it is like putting a shade on the lamp. Then you can see as far as the light reaches.

> Where the light does not reach, everything is dark, and you cannot see. Although there is a bad thing or affair beyond it, you cannot know it.[2]

Here we have an epistemological doctrine: knowledge involves the mind's projection of its illuminating capacity into the outer principles of things, thereby in turn increasing the clarity of its own comparable inner principles. But an ethical interest underlies the epistemology. This interest required that Zhu characterize the mind not only as a passive receiver of images or of information but also as capable of actively projecting itself into the objective world. With knowledge of things simultaneously comes sympathy toward them. This facilitates the knower's interest in aiding nature's nurturing process, to which I will turn in a moment.

Although the image of the mind containing its own light source plays a crucial role in Zhu Xi's quest for a means to unify self and things, it is insufficient by itself to explain cognition's tie to affect. This is because Zhu conceived of the experience of knowing as deeply affecting the entire self. The additional image that he used to expand the scope of the concept is that of a skeletal framework or a body (*ti*). When used as a verb in the context of relating the self to things, *ti* means to make things part of the body or of the self—in short, to embody them. *Tiren* means to understand something personally, with one's body and mind. This knowledge becomes qualitatively different from knowledge that does not involve personal experience. Investigating things goes beyond looking at static objects—it means getting involved with the affairs of the world. Embodiment is a combination of cognition (the light) and empathic projection of the self to the object (the body):

> Someone asked, "In the statement [of Zhang Zai], 'If there is a single thing that I have not embodied, then my mind has something outside of it,' what is the meaning of 'to embody'"? The answer was, "It means to put our minds into things and to investigate their principles, just as in investigating things and extending knowledge. It is different from the *ti* meaning substance that is paired with function.[3]

Chapter 4 identifies the "mirror neurons" that neuroscientists have discovered are the basis for our ability to empathize with other people. Today we would speak of having sympathy for what a person scientifically studies (a woodlot, a pond's fish population, an urban community). In the end, impartiality is both cognitive and affective. In referring to the cognitive, Cheng Yi puts it this way: "When one has no selfish subjectivity, there will be no occasion when he is acted on in which he will not respond to every stimulus with understanding."[4] The affective is explained this way: "The way of humaneness is difficult to describe; only the word impartiality comes close to it."[5] and "The humane man regards heaven, earth, and all things as one body; there is nothing not himself."

Confucianism provides powerful reasons for the preferential treatment of family members. And the family is the ultimate anchor of social stability. Social stability can be disrupted, however, if that care stops with the family, because, according to Zhu Xi, heaven and earth are concerned with the nourishment of all living things. Order will exist when humans cooperate with heaven and earth to that end, because order is a natural consequence of broadly oriented nurturance. I will now turn to the images of the plant and the gardener. These explain how the activities of knowing and loving fit into Zhu's view of the natural world. In his teachings, this fit guarantees their success.

THE PLANT AND THE GARDENER

The plant image as applied to the individual's mind reconciles the two values of family and universalistic love, making a place for both preferential and universal nurturance of others. It does so by treating the values as appropriate to different stages of the individual's own growth. In the early stages of development, the individual's efforts will be focused primarily on himself and his family. Assuming that development continues, the individual's capacity to nurture will expand beyond his family to other humans and creatures. Despite the individual's expanded concern, he must continue to function within the context of his various social roles, which he will never transcend. But with the proper nurturance, the individual's mind may grow progressively from love of kin to love of other people to love of other things in the world. Zhu describes the growth of the individual's mind this way:

> For instance, [the process] is like a grain of millet sprouting forth. Humaneness is the seed, filiality and brotherly love are the sprouts. Then humaneness is the root of filiality and brotherly love. ["Humaneness is the nature, filiality and brotherly love are the functions."] That is, it is like a tree having roots, a trunk, branches, and leaves. Loving one's parents is the root. Being humane to people is the trunk. Loving creatures is the branches and leaves. So practicing humaneness is based on taking filiality and brotherly love as the beginning.[6]

Also,

> A disciple asked about the difference between the mind, the nature, and the feelings. Zhu Xi replied, "Cheng Yi said, 'the mind is like the seed of grain; the principle of life in it is the nature; the yang material force in bringing forth life is the feelings.'"[7]

> A disciple asked, "The necessity that the seed of grain will grow is like the necessity for man to be humane. In this way we take growth as like humaneness. The life of the seed is the principle of growth. So then it follows that the principle of growth is humaneness." Zhu Xi replied, "It definitely must be so."[8]

The mind participates in the four-season growth cycle of plants (sprouting, development, fruition, and death/energy storage). The cycles apply to the entire life span of an individual's mind, as well as to moments within it. The growth process is present in the mind as potentiality, just as life lies hidden or dormant in the plant during winter or hidden in the seed before branches and leaves blossom forth.[9]

There is no conflict between the four seasons, so the humaneness is not in conflict with the earlier family oriented feelings.

CULTIVATING THE "SEED"

Recognition of the plantlike qualities of mind links respective duties with different stages of growth. Thereby Zhu precludes any conflict between duty to family and duty to the public. The target of nurturance becomes the self as the subject of self-cultivation, and other people, in a progressive sequence from within the kinship group to outside it. The plant image applies here.

One aspect of self-cultivation concerns actions before they are manifest, while they are still covert, private, and subjective. Zhu includes both overt conduct (*yifa*) and subjective stirrings to act (*weifa*) in the category of action, whether reference is to the individual, parent, official, or educator. Nurturing action while it is still not overt, a person can help ensure the propriety of its eventual manifestation. The language of the plant image informs the analysis, as Zhu explains that the *weifa* stage is one in which thoughts have not yet "budded forth."[10] Because there is one continuum from subjective thoughts to overt behavior, both are legitimate targets of self-cultivation and the instruction by other people, including officials. This is considerably different from the separation of belief and action in American culture for the past two centuries. In discussing religious beliefs, Thomas Jefferson wrote, "....that the legitimate powers of government reach actions only, and not opinions."[11]

Another aspect of self-cultivation is cleaning the mind of obstacles to growth and clarity, akin to weeding and watering. The weeds are the selfish desires. In many comparable Western approaches to ethics, at this stage the focus would instead be on choosing between alternative paths, for example the paths of reason and desire. But Zhu's underlying assumption is that with the removal of selfish desires comes automatic clarity of moral judgment and proper response according to the principles built into the mind. He provides a good illustration in his description of monks who leave their families and retreat to monasteries. Inevitably, they recreate familial relations in the temple, treating abbots as fathers and new monks as younger brothers.[12] Their quest for Paradise, salvation, or Nirvana is a selfish obstacle to development. It is implied that if the obstacles to their minds were eliminated, they would maintain proper relations at home in the first place and never leave for the monastery.

The cycle also applies to growth over a life-span. With the proper nurturance, the individual's mind may grow progressively from love of kin, to love of other people, to love of other things in the world. Recall the passage above,

> Loving one's parents is the root. Being humane to people is the trunk. Loving creatures is the branches and leaves. So practicing humaneness is based on taking filiality and brotherly love as the beginning.[13]

Zhu believes that in the expansive development of the mind's capacity for love, the beginning stage of a process—for example, love of kin—may have an intrinsic value that places it above being a simple means to an end. In contrast, Aristotle treats *full* actualization as the end (*telos*), and it is intrinsically more valuable than any earlier point in the process. Zhu could never accept that the early stages are mere means:

> Zhu Xi was asked if the statement that "filiality and brotherly love are the root of humaneness" means the following: having served your parents and elder brothers to the utmost, you have established the root, and then you expand it to loving other people and things; thereby your loving is practiced according to principle. Zhu Xi replied, "It is certainly so. But filiality and brotherly love are proper in themselves. It is not because you want to love people and love things that you then start with filiality and brotherly love."

Kexue said, "Would it be like a plant having its root, then the branches and foliage can be lush?" Zhu replied, "It is so, but where there is a root, the branch and foliage will naturally be lush. It is not because of the desire to have lush foliage that you then go to cultivate the root."[14]

In the end, when both the family love and love of others are present, we have a whole process. The process and then individual agent have integrity or sincerity (*cheng*):

"Integrity is something's beginning and end." Its origin is integrity, and its final point is also integrity. If there is integrity, then there is something substantial, and, if not, there is no substance.... For example, a plant from its germination until it withers, dies, and falls to the ground is following a real principle (*shili*).[15]

LIMITATIONS TO THE NOBLE VISION

Consider again the passage just above where Zhu Xi is asked about filiality and brotherly love being the root of humaneness. Zhu's position is that kinship love is intrinsically valuable yet simultaneously serves as a means. That is, cultivation of kinship love enhances one's ability to love others. But note the assumption. The progressive outward extension of affection to others is as natural as the stages from seed to ripened grain. The psychological implication is that being altruistic does not take much effort. Take care of the family love and the altruism will almost automatically follow. This may be a weak link in this ethics.

This is because it treats altruism as an inevitable byproduct of self-growth. The plant image does not require the individual to think about what specific method of outreach will work, because he believes his effort in the prior stages ensures satisfactory progress.

When the topic of altruism goes beyond the standard set of family relational roles, Zhu often treats it as an expectation for people at an advanced stage of moral growth, namely a small group of "parental officials." Only a small number of people could have identified with an audience of scholar-officials aspiring to *junzi* status. The low literacy rate would have restricted the size of this group.

From Zhu's memorials to the throne and from his letters, we gain an understanding of who the "people" are with whom he was in fact concerned. If the number of altruists is as small as the group of parental officials, there are also limits to the target group who are recipients of the welfare. The unit of primary welfare concern was the *xian* or county. Repeatedly he speaks in his memorials and letters of the need to attend to the poor at the county level by reducing their taxes. He wanted to lessen the gap between poor and rich counties. He referred to the masses inhabiting the counties as the "sons and daughters of the county magistrate."

Occasionally, in his educational materials and memorials, Zhu discusses altruism of ordinary people in smaller units, such as the community. He does this in his comments on the Lu family community contract (*xiangyue*) on which he did editorial work. The contract was an organizational model discussed or used at various times and locales in China to foster mutual encouragement for moral development among various families through periodic ceremonies, lectures, and public praise and criticism. Zhu says, for example, in the *Elementary Learning*, "When there is a calamity, all members of the community contract show sympathy for each other."[16] Showing sympathy is "aiding the sorrowful and needy." However, sympathy is not shown to people in general but to those with whom one has formed a relationship within the contract, that is people who participate in the ceremonies of the contract. In a public proclamation when he was magistrate, Zhu enjoined the people to show sympathy for members of their community in time of death, but, again, he was not promulgating a general ethical principle that was to be treated as universally applicable.

EVALUATION

There is a difference between Zhu's idea of altruism and the standards by which someone in the twenty-first century might be tempted to judge him. If we take account of historical context, however, we are left with a positive evaluation of Zhu as an individual. He was a person of compassion. He even advocated forcing the wealthy to help the poor in times of emergency. [17] As an official, he compiled an admirable record in famine relief and the establishment of communal granaries. In a memorial he advised the emperor to issue an edict encouraging granaries in other areas than his own. Zhu left a fine legacy of support for schools and the design of curricular materials. Robert Hymes has argued that in supporting the community contract, local academies, and communal granaries (no interest charges on loans to farmers at planting time), Zhu and other officials were trying to fill a gap left by a weakened central authority.

That authority had lost strength fighting with and paying off the invaders from the north.[18]

In going as far as he did in advocating an altruistic attitude, Zhu was remarkably broader in concern than those in the mainstream of his social group. All we need to do is look at examples of others from his class at the time. Robert Hymes has described the arguments that several persons used to justify charity. The brother of the philosopher Lu Jiuyuan argued from utility that one should give to the needy rather than fear conflict with those who expect that one should do it. Charity was a consideration, but it ranked below preservation of family property. Hymes wrote, "The use of such arguments from self-interest suggests that there was con-siderable disagreement as to the ethical basis—or more broadly, the basis in general rules of social behavior—of charity in general and relief grain sales in particular."[19] Patricia Ebrey's study of Yuan Cai (1140–1195) reveals that many members of Zhu's class treated fear of loss of prosperity as paramount. Thus preservation of the property of the individual's own family was the ultimate value, rather than universal love of "people and creatures."[20] The historical record indicates that the power and greed of rich families within clans acted to fragment even a clan organization, when one existed.

Here we have examples of the ties of emotion and thought. People such as Mr. Lu and Mr. Yuan had been taught about the fact that *tiandao* is concerned with the nurturance of all people. They had learned the value of charity and altruism from the *Doctrine of the Mean* and from the metaphysics of the Cheng brothers. But the emotion of fear of conflict or of property loss was mixed with what they learned. So good education and thinking do not guarantee comparable results in action.

People can control their emotions by controlling what books they read or with which friends they choose to associate. They can choose to prolong sympathy by attention and memory. Zhu Xi gives guidance on that score. But this still leaves charity and welfare to the individual's choice. I do not trust individuals alone with the care of non kin or non-neighbors. There must be enforced laws that guarantee nurturance or the weak and manifest a belief in the equal worth of all. We know this today. Zhu did not know it then.

It is certainly true that Zhu never dealt with the problem of balancing competing interests of different groups, including those within the clan. But clarity about the nature of groups and their competing interests did not begin even in the West until the advent of the social sciences in the nineteenth century. I propose that we build on the wisdom of the past, beginning with this knowledge from the social sciences.

From the perspective of time, Zhu Xi was an exemplary symbol of what he preached. We need to dip into new knowledge that we possess from our modern age to find the best supplements to his theory of balancing family love and altruism beyond the family. One of these sources is game theory, many studies of which center on the Prisoner's Dilemma. There is rich material in these studies as a basis for policies. They demonstrate that among genetically unrelated people, reciprocal altruism can be preserved as the value of cooperation, because it may be beneficial to all parties. Cooperation is a virtue consistent with Confucian communitarianism and altruism. It requires that individuals, groups, and nations give up a bit of their own autonomy or sovereignty. Within their respective domains, genes, families, villages, and religious organizations share interests with others, which is why seeking a win-win or non-zero-sum situation for conflict resolution works within them. Success depends on sharing of information relevant to their common interests. Part of that information concerns what each side is willing to give up for the benefit of all on both sides. Of course, knowledge about these studies is not sufficient by itself to facilitate conflict resolution. It must be knowledge in the hands of those who agree with it and who have some power to use it.

Today we also add to Zhu Xi's agenda the law. Because most people will show preferential affection for their kin, the ultimate safety net for nurturing care for others is laws and their enforcement. These are laws that protect and provide for those other people in ways that we ourselves may not provide. In the United States a great deal has been learned about such laws over the decades since Franklin Roosevelt introduced Social Security legislation in the 1930s. He assumed that some individuals will not make choices consistent with their long term welfare, so the law does it for them. China's 1995 Education Law is another modern example. But in addition to law, there must be public and official respect for enforcing the law.

After considering all of these additions from modern knowledge, there remains an insight of Zhu Xi the importance of which Western social scientists and legal scholars have not grasped. It is equally as significant as any of the modern additions in its utility for achieving stable and caring societies. This is that at the very end (even after cooperation based on shared interests is achieved), the goal is a new style of relationship between the parties. The relationship involves an emotional bond, reinforced by rituals, that goes beyond the mere acts of cooperation.[21]

We can retain our respect for Zhu Xi's contributions to the theory of universal altruism and to its status as an ideal to be sought through cultivating sympathy and knowledge together. This has been a powerful motive to some people's actions, including the famous Confucian Generals who put down the Taiping Rebellion. Drawing on modern information about groups, game theory applied to cooperation, law, and positive education about law, we try to increase the likelihood of a transition from Zhu's noble ideal to reality.

3

Lecture Three:
Two Kinds of Models and the Value
of Autonomy

We teach people to be good citizens and we teach them to solve society's technical problems. Over the centuries, Chinese scholars have advocated using models as instructional aides in both cases. But a style of teaching that trains people to be good citizens may not be a good style for training people to solve technically complex problems. Presenting models may work in the transmission of values, but may not work in the study of data analysis.[1]

CHARACTER MODELS

Confucian scholars discovered very early that in moral education, model emulation is not just one way of learning; it is by far the most efficient way. The early writings on model emulation reveal acute psychological insights valid in any culture and any historical era. This is especially true for their insights about socialization of children. Educational texts and historical writings are filled with positive and negative models. Guan Yu was the model of loyalty, Shun the model of filiality. There were many local exemplars too. Ever since those early days, Chinese educators have known that people learn ethical practices or consciousness of a moral sense from adults in large part through what Westerners call "observational learning," that is, observing a model in reality or in stories.

In the classical formulation, "teaching by example surpasses teaching by words" (*shenjiao sheng yu yanjiao*). Sometimes models were exemplary people from the past, such as ancestors or sages whose exploits are recorded in writings. Sometimes a model was a living person, such as a father, teacher, official, or ruler. The Master remarked, "When one sees a worthy, one should think of equaling him."[2] Cultivated persons have an obligation to serve as models for others to emulate. Confucius said that "When those who are in high stations perform well all their duties to their relations, the people are aroused to virtue."[3] And *The Great Learning* adds, "When the ruler, as a father, a son, and a brother is a model, then the people imitate him."[4]

In practice, in the Confucian tradition, respect, which comes from being imitated, is preferred as an incentive to material rewards. The opportunity to influence others, not material advantage, was supposed to be the goal of those who sought official position. Those exemplary officials who were unmindful of personal gain while in office were "pure officials" (*qingguan*).

Starting in the early Zhou period, model emulation was one of two contending methods of social control. On one side were the Confucians, advocating control by the presentation of models, whose inner attitudes and behaviors would be emulated by the people and made habitual. Thereby, for them, doing the right things would be spontaneous. On the other side were the statesmen who advocated universally applicable penal laws, which controlled people primarily through fear of punishment. The Master said,

> If the people be led by laws, and uniformity sought to be given them by punishments, they will try to avoid the punishment, but have no sense of shame. If they be led by virtue [*de*], and uniformity sought to be given them by the rules of propriety, they will have a sense of shame, and moreover will become good.[5]

The argument is that law controls through fear of punishment; it does not change people's attitudes or habits. As a result, in the words of an ancient treatise, the people "come to have a contentious spirit, and make their appeal to the express words of the law, hoping peradventure to be successful in their argument." That is to say, people will do everything they can to get around the wording of the law rather than submit to its spirit. Furthermore, since people's attitudes and habits are not changed, they will disobey the law whenever the policeman is not around. For this reason and others, Confucian thought prefers to transform or control by the presentation of virtuous models. People will emulate them and develop a constant attitude toward the rules, which will ensure proper conduct even when no one is around.[6] This use of moral models has continued into modern China. During the Maoist period, most Chinese were exposed to the noble deeds of Lei Feng, Ouyang Hai, and Wang Jie.

And they learned character failings through the negative models Li Lisan and Lin Biao.

Teaching character development through models is especially congenial to communitarian societies such as exist in China. A community may be a place in which people have the same legal residence, voting rights, or tax obligations. It is a place where there is some overlap of individual and group interests. Social relations are generally stable and behavior somewhat predictable. The existence of shared values makes it possible to achieve consensus on what is acceptable and unacceptable conduct. In this situation, the ultimate sanctions for observance or non-observance of community standards exemplified in the models are group sanctions, either peer respect or peer ostracism.

PROBLEM SOLVING MODELS

At the same time that models have served well the goal of socializing the youth, they have also been used for another goal, where they have often been an obstruction. That other goal is to teach problem solving by copying models as a method of inquiry and data analysis. In pre-modern China this meant studying the texts of the sages in order to learn about the archetypal situations they described. In the twelfth century, Zhu Xi wrote, "We learn the *dao* of the sages so we can know the mind of the sages. When we know the mind of the sages and use that to manage our minds to the point where they are no different from that of the sage, this is what is called the transmission of the mind."[7]

Often committed to memory, these situational models were considered archetypal of actual cases. Some of these were models of organizations or institutions associated with a morally exemplary utopian age, such as the institutions of the early Zhou regime. Many were laid out in the *Four Books* or in the *Rites of Zhou* (*Zhouli*). One example is the well-field (*jingtian*) system of land allocation and taxation idealized in the *Mencius*. The same applies to various practices in the *Rites of Zhou* that were subsequently advocated by Wang Anshi and others, such as eliminating the division of labor between farmers and police. Obstruction of inquiry arose because the attention of the later investigators was shifted away from the objective current case and projected instead onto a preexisting, formulaic textual situation. Let me give one example.

In the late sixteenth century, as Ray Huang has described it, problems faced by the central government included unpaid officials, the absence of money to finance a strong army, and a lack of funds to repair dikes for flood control.

> Although it recognized these undesirable conditions, the court in the later period was helpless to provide a fundamental cure for them. The dynasty had followed the vision of the *Four Books* too closely to consider other approaches. Adjudging simple living a permanent national characteristic, the bureaucratic apparatus had deliberately been constructed to avoid technical complexities.... The Civil Service had neither the administrative expertise nor the necessary service facilities to allow itself to keep pace with a national economy that was expanding in both size and degree of sophistication.[8]

Tax quotas had not been revised in two hundred years; assessments did not correspond to holdings, as rich districts had low tax quotas. The *Four Books* did not provide a suitable model for solving a problem of that sixteenth century age, namely financial reform. Those classics by the sages provided primarily the model of frugal officials. But this model, plus the usual obstructions by vested interests, meant that the state income was too low to pay for its operations. The Civil Service salary scale was so low that many officials received almost no salary. The policy of frugality could not fill the treasury, drive away invaders, or repair dikes. Failure to cope with the military and water control problems were two of several factors that weakened the dynasty. In the middle of the next century it collapsed. In short, with archetypal or situational models, there is often no attempt to select a model that matches in specific details the person or situation with the current problem.

Just as the successful use of virtuous models for character transformation continued into the modern period, symbolized by Lei Feng, so did the less effective use of models for solving complex problems exemplified in this late Ming illustration. These latter models were part of the Leader's pursuit of the value of one-mindedness for the country as a whole. The models promote uniformity of thought in dealing with problems, rather than the solicitation of a rich variety of proposed solutions.

I will cite two examples. The first is the possible population problem, identified in 1957 by the social scientist Ma Yinchu, then president of Peking University, and a member of the National People's Congress. Based on empirical studies that he led from 1953 to 1955, (field trips in Zhejiang, material gathered from Jiangxi, Shanxi, Shandong, Jiangsu, Shanghai, and Beijing,) he published his final findings as *The New Theory of Population* (*Xin renkou lun*). His basic point was that the rate of population growth was increasing greater than the capacity for capital accumulation, impeding China's development. His proposals: a two-child family, late marriage, contraception, and so forth. At this time, China was following the Soviet model in solving socio-economic problems. But the Soviets used unreliable statistics and claimed great increases in production in the years after World War II ended, and those supposed increases coexisted with an open ended population growth. The Soviets had outlawed abortion in 1936 and in 1944 introduced rewards for fertile mothers and taxes on the childless to promote population growth. There were no controls on population growth. To follow the Soviet model in China was to affirm two values, obedience to the Leader's orders to copy the U.S.S.R., and faith in Chinese people's effort or will to overcome production problems. Understandably, both Mao and Liu Shaoqi attacked Ma for underestimating the power of the people's enthusiasm to raise productivity. Ma was fired, lost his membership in the Standing Committee of the National People's Congress, and was thrown into the Chinese gulag. Years later, many of Ma's facts were found to be relevant to formulating policy about the population increases.[9]

On September 14, 1979, the Central Committee of the Chinese Communist Party reversed its resolution of twenty years before that had condemned Ma.[10] The author of his 1986 biography wrote that had his analysis been accepted, the population would have been smaller by 250,000,000. In preferring the Soviet model to Ma's research facts until the 1970s, China's leaders had chosen a model that masked the differences between the factual situation in the two sites for its application. The wonders of production increase they had attributed to the Soviet Union had actually been unsubstantiated. And there was no comparison between the huge loss of population in the U.S.S.R. in the War, justifying incentives for fertility, and that in China.

Another example. In 1979 the inland Daqing oil fields in Heilongjiang province still served as a model for industrial production, just as Dazhai did for farming. These units provided models of production processes and also demonstrated the miracles that a proper attitude toward goals could achieve. At this time, Bohai No. 2 was the name of an offshore drilling platform that had been purchased from abroad at considerable expense. The officials in the Ministry of Petroleum who were in charge of Bohai No. 2 had taken Daqing as their model regardless of the fact that Daqing's operation bore little resemblance to oil platform production.

In November, 1979, the platform was being towed from a previous site to a new one in the Gulf of the Bohai off China's northeast coast. The team on the platform was entitled to receive information about water depth, undersea land formation, bottom sediment, and current weather reports. The Ministry officials on land were imitating the Daqing model. They ignored the differences between it and the ocean oil platform, and sent none of the required reports to the platform on the water and weather conditions. On the morning of November 25, 1979, under the impact of a force-ten wind, Bohai No. 2 capsized, drowning 72 of the 74 team members aboard and destroying an enormous investment in the platform itself. A *People's Daily* editorial of August, 1980 stated that the problem lay with the Petroleum Ministry's copying old modes of action and not paying attention to what was different about the Bohai case: the machinery was new and nothing like that at Daqing; the work was at sea and not on land. Confidence in "subjective initiative" or people's effort had facilitated dismissal of obvious relevant and critical facts needed by the platform team, according to the final report.[11]

SCIENTIFIC INQUIRY AND AUTONOMY: THE ALTERNATIVE TO ANTECEDENT MODELS

In solving technical problems, there is an alternative to copying antecedent complex models promoted by authorities with their own value agendas. It is scientific inquiry. Such inquiry is not value free. The point is that the values must be ones that permit rather than obstruct self-correcting views about facts. Inquiry must be protected from domineering control by something other than the world itself. Jurgen Habermas has proposed that certain values are privileged, namely those that promote communication, sharing of information, and the absence of coercion. Simplicity and fruitfulness in generating other hypotheses are values for innovation. I would add to the list individual autonomy of judgment by those concerned with finding solutions to social problems.

When the value of individual autonomy has legitimacy, a multitude of individuals will feel free and motivated to put forth their own hypotheses when they study a problem. Autonomy, therefore, is a necessary condition for variability in theories. Where there is variability, people learn from each other. Among competing theories, some will prevail. This approach opposes single models and single authorities for complex problems, such as those presented by political or community leaders. It does not oppose the authority of peers, however. Because the individual's particular prejudices may affect his theories, there is a place for the authority of peer evaluation and correction.

There is evidence that now is the time in which the value of autonomy is making an appearance in China. This evidence lies in the striking convergence since the early 1980s of interests in both elite theory and popular media (especially in the latter) around the single theme of autonomy. My guess about the timing is that it has had to do with the emergence of individual and local entrepreneurial agents in the free market economy. Entrepreneurs prize the right to decide which beliefs motivate their lives and affect their balance sheets. Translators usually render the English word "autonomy" as *zizhu* (self-master) or *zizhi* (self-in-control). However in theoretical and popular contexts, several other terms appear where the English speaker would use "autonomy": *duli sikao* (independent thinking) and *nengdongxing* (initiative), for example.

In elite theory discussed by professional educators and philosophers, the technical context in which autonomy emerged for discussion was *zhutixing* (subjectivity). The focus of these educators is on the subject or individual actor helping to create something new in his work rather than being a passive recipient of stimuli. Theorists envisioned it as the individual choosing or acting as an agent with some independence of official culture. The topic of subjectivity fits easily into that central interest of Confucian philosophy, the theory of human nature. "Human subjectivity is the part of human nature which expresses man's essence in the most concentrated way; it is the quintessence of human nature."[12] Assigned to human nature, subjectivity as the ability and desirability of the individual acting autonomously, attains an elevated status, in these works over the past two decades. Professor Tze-wan Kwan has identified the Western interest in subjectivity, a precursor to that in China. He traces it to Descartes, for whom the self or subject is central to having knowledge. In contrast to the positive reception of the idea of subjectivity in China, Kwan highlights Heidegger's warning in the West that subjectivity can involve treating things as mere objects in our quest for knowledge, placing them at the whim of our manipulation. This can lead to ecological and social crises, which may be avoided when things are also the object of some affection and respect, as Zhu Xi would teach.[13]

Autonomy also entered the mainstream of urban popular youth culture as part of the rediscovery of the self. Some of the most compelling evidence for this can be found in a series of articles in the journal *China Youth* in 1980 and two overview studies in the same journal, one in 1988 and another in 1992 that summed up developments of the previous years on this topic. The movement appeared in public with the journal's original request for opinion on the subject of the self. They received some 60,000 letters by young people daring to express their beliefs in print. Factory workers, farmers, commercial people, students, and soldiers all wrote to the editors. The 1992 article says that a new era in the study of the self has arrived with the popularization of ideas that had been in circulation since 1980. "Seven or eight years ago 'the self,' to a very significant degree, was an abstract 'theory'…" centering on such ideas as self-design, self-realization, independence, and knowing the self. However, now, the author continues, "'the theory' has already become conventional wisdom." It is simply assumed that individuals should choose their own future course (*xuanze ziji de qiantu*). The convention now also includes the belief that, "My choice may not be approved by everyone, but I believe that it is the most valuable." This theme flourished in popular short stories and novels.[14]

WHY AUTONOMY EMERGES[15]

In addition to the economic factors I have already mentioned (the demands of entrepreneurs), there are historical and philosophical developments that promote a climate in which autonomy as a value can grow. The historical ones concern the emergence of organizations separate from the state that try to protect their members ability to voice and pursue certain common interests. In the West, this occurred in sixteenth and seventeenth century Europe with religious congregations demanding toleration of their beliefs by the state. For example, the predecessors of the modern day Unitarians affirmed that every person must be permitted to determine by himself which parts of the New Testament are accessible to reason and which are matters of faith. Eventually in the West the momentum that began in religious congregations for freedom of religious belief evolved into political and philosophical arguments for freedom of belief on all matters.

This historical condition did not exist in China until recently. Imperial Confucianism treated the emperor as the intermediary between heaven and humans. All humans and their organizations were subordinate to the emperor, who sought a condition of "one-mindedness" throughout the realm. There was no direct line from the individual to Heaven, the Buddha, or Laozi that could circumvent the emperor as the state, the ultimate arbiter of acceptable beliefs on all matters. Religious congregations (*hui*) with heterodox beliefs did exist and operated apart from the state, in the village and more widely (such as the White Lotus Society). But from time to time these communities were viewed as a threat by the state, which never gave up its position that the emperor is the ultimate standard and model for all minds. Even nonreligious organizations in late imperial times, such as merchant guilds, operated successfully only with official patronage. And today, all groups must maintain relations with official agencies in order to function; they are called "affiliated units" (*guagou danwei*).

Nevertheless, the recent emergence of nongovernmental organizations (NGOs) in China with weak ties to governmental agencies represents a crucial development toward the toleration of plurality of beliefs, such as the religious congregations in Europe helped to foster. There was a real burgeoning of their numbers in the 1980s. Examples from the 1990s include Project Hope, part of the China Youth Development foundation, the Yunnan Minorities and Gender Development Group, and the Institute for Ecological Conservation and Development in Kunming. Even more important than the NGOs themselves would be the existence of laws that protect people in them when they express opinions that run contrary to official positions, and also oversight agencies that ensure that the laws are applied. There should also be a further weakening of the requirement of "affiliated unit" status.

Philosophically, the major step toward the emergence of autonomy as a value is an idea first majestically described by Wang Yangming in China and by Kant in the West. This is that the individual is the ultimate authority on general moral rules. Wang stated,

> In innate knowledge and innate ability, men and women of simple intelligence and the sage are equal. Their difference lies in the fact that the sage alone can extend [act on] his innate knowledge…"[16]

Kant said that every rational being is his own legislator of normative principles.

But both thinkers, Wang Yangming and Kant, agreed on another point that served to undercut their advance toward a modern idea of autonomy. Their idea was that all clear-header people think alike. For Wang, the mind that people share is the same; it does not possess individual and innate differences. For Kant, logic requires that all rational people will discover the same things to be duties.

I argue that as long as autonomy is paired with this idea that all people who think correctly will think alike, the philosophical door is open to authorities who can undercut the force of autonomy. This is because some people will claim that others do not think rationally or clearly. Therefore, those who do think clearly can legitimately think for the others, since, if rational, they would come to the same conclusion. So the others need paternalistic supervision. Both Kant and Republican China stressed the need for a period of tutelage over the people, before full autonomy is granted.

This idea of all rational or clear-headed people thinking alike began to breakdown in the West under the impact of the German Romantics in nineteenth century Europe. They glorified each individual's unique inner resources and ability to turn away from popular culture. Among them was Wilhelm von Humboldt, who J. S. Mill explicitly credits in *On Liberty*. Freedom of choice must be allowed "to unfold freely in both thought and practice...."[17] In China, the beginnings of acceptance of individual choice in matters of belief are already there with the subjectivity movement and in popular culture.

So the value of autonomy of judgment is the best alternative to the reflexive reliance on antecedent models for solving technical problems. Hopefully, it is beginning to grow in China, though it needs changes in the affiliated status of NGOs, as well as laws that protect open discussion of problem solving issues and oversight agencies that ensure the laws are observed as intended. Chad Hansen has suggested that it might also help to allow a multitude of competing typical models for solving the same general type of problem.

There may always be some hidden impediments to full autonomy in the form of advertizing and political messages in the media, a situation found in most developed countries, with some burden falling on the individual to sort these out.

CONCLUSION

In evaluating the dual role of models in Chinese views about knowledge, it is essential to distinguish between premises as they apply to problem solving inquiry and to what Confucians have called self-cultivation. In the case of the former, models of complex organizations, situations, or policies that contain detailed recipes for an investigator to follow (such as the Daqing oil fields) stand a good chance of not being useful in the search for solutions to problems. There is too much room for slippage between the structure of the model and the circumstances under study.

But I applaud with vigor the benefits from models for character development. These benefits include self-discipline, self-development, and community order. People do effectively learn to do the right thing by emulating models. We call them role models, and psychologists call the procedure observational learning. From them we learn the standards of right and wrong and an inner attitude that gives us a commitment to do the right thing. To be single-minded in commitment to a value is a form of willpower that can give the individual an edge. Those who practice the martial arts know that concentrating on one thing and avoiding distractions focuses the energy needed to succeed. Discipline involves mindfulness of and acceptance of a standard. When there is a convergence of what a person has to do and of what he believes is right, there can be spontaneity in moral action. Although spontaneity is rarely a virtue in technical inquiry, it may very well be a virtue in routine ethical behavior. The neurologist Antonio Damasio has tracked the relation between an emotional stimulus (with which emulated models are endowed) and alterations in the decision-making process:

> It can produce alterations in working memory, attention, and reasoning so that the decision-making process is biased toward selecting the action most likely to lead to the best possible outcome, given prior experience. The individual may not ever be cognizant of this covert operation. In these conditions, we intuit a decision and enact it, speedily and efficiently, without any knowledge of the intermediate steps.[18]

Models that exemplify concretely simple character traits or attitudes are often effective in transforming social behavior. This is especially the case if individuals wish to change, as do those receptive to Confucian teachings on self-cultivation. Models, moral spontaneity, and concern for group judgment have played a positive role in nurturing the steadfast Confucian heroes who inspire many Chinese. These include Wang Yangming.

So while I advocate the replacement of the reflexive reliance on models in technical inquiry with such epistemic values as autonomy, I also champion the maintenance of model-driven forms of character training that endure from the past. There is room for both individual judgment and the emulation of moral models in modern China.

PART B

A Chinese Ethics for the New Century

4

The Biological Basis of Confucian Ethics: Or, A Reason Why Confucianism Has Endured for So Long

INTRODUCTION

I have long been interested in trying to answer the question: Why has the legacy of Mencian inspired Confucianism endured for so long? I believe that the answer includes the fact that much of it is consistent with the human condition. Ethical principles must be consistent with human nature in order for people to find them compelling and motivating. Otherwise, they will be alienated from those principles. The only social policies that have a reasonable chance of long term success are those compatible with human nature. Recall the failure of the late 1950s Maoist attempt to force Chinese into communal dining at the expense of family bonds. A version of utilitarianism also fails, because it says that in measuring the cost/benefits of our actions each person affected counts for the same one unit, even if they are our close family members. Advocates of Confucianism who wish others to treat it seriously should remember to underscore this fortunate feature about its ethics, that in many ways it is not alienating. They should emphasize that the ethics has some biological basis.

Some Westerners may wish to anchor their ethics in beliefs about a divine design in the universe or the commands of God. Similarly, many Confucians may wish to anchor their ethical principles in beliefs about a

---

* This essay is a synthesis and summary of material first developed in the essays found in Chapters 5, 6 and 7. But those chapters also contain substantive additional material not found here. Some portions originally appeared in *Dao: A Journal of Comparative Philosophy*, 1.2 (2002), pp. 131–141.

heavenly way (*tiandao*) or in the belief that human nature comes from Heaven. This is certainly consistent with the Confucian tradition. There are psychological and aesthetic benefits of such beliefs. They may cause us to prize the world we live in or the people in it. I have no objection to people taking this position. It is compatible with the biological positions that the Mencian Confucians also maintain. I would argue, however, that those Chinese ethicists who wish to join the international discourse on values would be advised to focus on the biological, not the heavenly. The latter is likely to be both unclearly understood and minimally engaging for the international audience.

For some people, to hear the word "biological" in this context is to hear a warning. That warning alerts them to be on guard against any reductionist theory. This would be a theory that voids free will by tracing all human actions to biological causes over which the individual has no control. But I make no reductionist claim. I believe that there are behavioral tendencies. The Confucian position focuses on built-in tendencies toward certain patterns of behavior. One such tendency is toward recognizing and acting in accordance with the power of sympathy and cooperation, both in the case of kin and of out-groups. It is quite compatible with free will, where free will means that the individual is also capable of making uncaused choices. Here "uncaused" means uncoerced. Those choices may involve acting contrary to a tendency that is biologically favored, as in Steven Pinker's example below of the individual deciding against having children, though biologically the act of reproduction may be pleasant. Just because you know your tendencies does not mean you are locked into them.

Some prominent philosophers and anthropologists in the West currently argue against any meaningful idea of human nature. The American philosopher Richard Rorty (*Truth and Progress*) says that we should stop asking what our nature is and instead ask, "What can we make of ourselves?"[1] Certain anthropologists, beginning with the aim of discrediting hereditary differences among ethnic groups, end by rejecting any idea of an innate human nature.[2] In contrast, the Confucian position affirms an inborn nature, and in so doing is reinforced by the findings of contemporary evolutionary biology. The Confucians derive premises from the *Mencius* position that there are universal human emotions and thoughts, plus predispositions to act in accordance with them. So Confucians and the biologists agree that there is a human nature. The biologists assume that the predispositions and social emotions that form human nature contribute to the survival of individual or group genes, a topic absent from the Confucian case.

FROM INFANT-LOVE TO ALTRUISM

They also share beliefs about its content. The first is that love or sympathy, which originate among kin, are universal traits, being the subjective forms in which we experience altruism. "Filiality and brotherly love are the root of humaneness," the *Analects* (1.2) had said. The *Mencius* had referred to the "Five Relations," the first of which is that "Between father and son, there should be affection."[3] I take it that this formulation is the gender-biased symbol of the innate emotional bond between caregiver and child; most evolutionary biologists view it as innate and universal, with a maternal figure as the usual caregiver. Mencius certainly argues that we must have the right moral will in order to behave properly. But he also believes in our inborn tendencies to so act. Herein lies the biological basis to his ethics. His claim in this passage is both descriptive and prescriptive: we are the kind of people who by nature experience affection between father and son, and also we should express it. Further, the text says that the gentleman first treats his kin as kin, and then treats the people with humaneness.[4] It also says that "Loving one's kin is humaneness."[5] Zhu Xi (1130–1200) says that kinship love is natural and proper. He also goes on to say that love of other people and things beyond the immediate family develop when this kinship love exists. The modern biologists also explain altruism as similarly derived from kinship love. They define it as behavior, rooted in emotions, that benefits another person at a cost to the provider of the benefits, greater than any benefit the provider receives.

Although there may be some culturally universal human traits, the evolutionary psychologist is interested in those patterns of social emotions and related behavior that have genetic roots. He also recognizes that the genes interact with the environment, resulting in some variable behavior. Most writers agree on the existence of at least this biologically based trait: sympathy, which grows out of the infant-caregiver relation, and certain other associated emotions, described in the citations below. The sociobiologist Edward O. Wilson puts it this way:

> Among the traits with documented heritability, those closest to moral aptitude are empathy to the distress of others and certain processes of attachment between infants and their caregivers. To the heritability of moral

aptitude add the abundant evidence of history that cooperative individuals generally survive longer and leave more offspring. It is to be expected that in the course of evolutionary history, genes predisposing people toward cooperative behavior would have come to predominate in the human population as a whole.

Such a process repeated through thousands of generations inevitably gave birth to the moral sentiments. With the exception of stone psychopaths (if any truly exist), these instincts are vividly experienced by every person variously as conscience, self-respect, remorse, empathy, humility, and moral outrage.[6]

Kin selection [acting beneficially on behalf of individual kin] is the natural selection of genes based on their effects on individuals carrying them plus the effects the presence of genes has on all the genetic relatives of the individuals, including parents, siblings, cousins, and others who still live and are capable either of reproducing or of affecting the reproduction of blood relatives. Kin selection is especially important in the origin of altruistic behavior.[7]

To the above list, some also add the emotional bias against incest, and the aversion to pain coupled with a receptivity to pleasure.

So this is the first position on which the Confucian and biologist can agree: child-caregiver love, normally beginning in the family, is the root of altruism, and both are universal emotions. All kinds of differences separate the Confucian and the biologist or psychologist. For example, the latter find altruism beginning in the behavior of elders to younger kin. This is consistent with the Mencius example of an adult's predictable reaction to a child about to fall into a well; but in the patriarchal Confucian view of the duty of children to attend to their elder parents, the emphasis is sometimes on the reverse, the duties of the young to the elders. The subject for the biologist is genes and what makes them successfully reproduce, rather than the occupants of social roles (such as father-son). And Confucian references to universal traits probably contain a pro-male gender bias. But the Confucian and the biologist still share the fundamental positions, of which this first is: altruism begins in the family and spreads outward. Along with Confucians, I also share the view that family is not just the beginning of altruism but also has a first priority in the allocation of my resources and care.

Altruistic acts toward relatives promote the reproduction of the genes of the benefactor. Altruistic acts are often a function of the degree of relatedness or of shared genes. One of the most common forms of altruism is the sharing of information that facilitates survival. This information may be directly related to physical survival, such as guidance about available food, water or shelter, or the presence of threatening outsiders. It also may include information about kinship categories.

RECIPROCAL ALTRUISM

The second shared position between the Confucian and evolutionary biologist or psychologist is that altruism is reciprocal. The essence of Confucian altruism is that it is reciprocal. Starting in the Zhou period, there were two terms that refer to reciprocity. One is *de* (virtue, kindness). Those who practice *de* find that it is reciprocated, as in the statement, "There is no kindness that is not requited (*wu de bu bao*)."[8] The character *de* (kindness) was often associated with the character *de* (to get). The early bronze inscriptions have many references to the fact that the ruler who treats the people with *de* receives in return their affection and future loyal service (I discuss this in the Appendix to *The Concept of Man in Early China*). This same *de* became part of pre-Qin Confucian ethics.

The other term is *shu*, meaning that a person should use his own feelings as a guide in treating others, not doing to others what he would not want done to himself. This is the one principle to guide every daily act.[9] In seeking to cultivate themselves, persons seek to embody those virtues. In addition to reciprocity being involved in these basic virtues, it is also reinforced by the relational categories in terms of which people are instructed to think of themselves and others. This is an application of the family analogy to all persons who partake of one or more relational social roles, beginning with the basic "Five Relations" mentioned above: father-son, prince-minister, husband-wife, elder brother-younger brother, and friend-friend. Each person has duties to and legitimate beneficial expectations from the other party in the set.

Note that reciprocal altruism extends altruism beyond the kinship group, though its evolutionary basis is similar to kin selection. But it includes non-kin as well as kin. The main point is that the benefits are received by persons who are more likely to reciprocate or return the favor than are random persons in the population. The seminal biological work on reciprocal altruism was done in 1971 by Robert Trivers, building on the 1964 work of William D. Hamilton. Trivers states that "The pre-condition for the evolution of reciprocal altruism are similar to those for the operation of kin selection...."[10] Trivers and others have identified numerous examples of reciprocal altruism among birds, fish, dolphins, primates, bats, and impalas. For example, with respect to the warning calls of birds, Trivers notes:

> Thus, it seems that giving a warning call must result, at least occasionally, in the otherwise unnecessary death of the call-giver, either at the hands of the predator that inspired the call or at the hands of a second predator formerly unaware of the caller's presence or exact location.[11]

Natural selection favors the spread of the warning-call genes, increasing the likelihood of the benefit being reciprocated to the advantage of the initial caller or its kin. The warnings prevent predators from specializing only on the caller's species and locale. The survival of neighboring birds repays the altruism of the call-giver, whose genetic kind may be saved by the future calls of the surviving birds.

For the biologist, the outward spread of altruism among humans has been described in this way, "A gene that repaid kindness with kindness could thus have spread through the extended family, and, by interbreeding, to other families, where it would thrive on the same logic."[12] Among genetically unrelated people, reciprocal altruism can be preserved as the value of cooperation, because it is beneficial to all parties. Cooperation is a virtue consistent with Confucian communitarianism and altruism. Recall E. O. Wilson's comment that "cooperative individuals generally survive longer and leave more offspring." The biologist Trivers incorporates these findings in his own work.

Some writers state that the principal condition required for the reciprocating of acts of kindness is "a stable, repetitive relationship." [13] This is the kind of relationship in which people come to know each other's likely behavior. It is also the kind in which the sharing of information, basic to successful cooperation, is common. It is epitomized in Confucian role relationships.

EMOTIONS AND MORAL REASONING

There is a third principle shared by the Confucian and the evolutionary biologist or psychologist. It is that moral concepts owe much more to innate social emotions than Western psychologists or ethicists have traditionally recognized. The Confucian position is illustrated in the description of one of the "four minds" identified by Mencius. It is *shifei zhi xin* (the mind of right and wrong). This phrase says both that this mind can know (a cognitive matter) right and wrong, and, simultaneously, that it will approve of right and disapprove of wrong (the emotional acceptance or rejection). These emotions are the motives for action. Hence, Confucians developed the principle of "the unity of knowledge and action," because emotionally charged knowledge motivates action.

To return to the general topic of moral reasoning, today we know this. Whether the topic is emotions that are culturally molded in content or emotions in their innate form, they play a crucial role in the individual's moral deliberation. If the content of people's emotions differ because of their backgrounds, they will think differently about what is right or wrong.[14] Great strides in Western cognitive and brain science of the past thirty years have disturbed our old Western ideas about the mind by revealing that there are no clear-cut divisions between psychological "faculties." The traditional Platonic view holds that thinking or reasoning is most successful when it is free of the emotions, which introduce bodily distractions into its activity. Emotions are treated as generally negative, always needing to be controlled by reason. Nowadays that position has faded in the West, replaced by the claim that cognition, emotions, and motives are all interrelated. Furthermore, in emotions and motives lie the keys to moving from a knowledge of what is, to doing something about it.

Neurologist Antonio Damasio recently noted, "The presumed opposition between emotion and reason is no longer accepted without question...emotion is integral to the processes of reason and decision-making, for worse and for better."[15] He continues with the comment that emotions have a regulatory role, leading to circumstances advantageous to the organism, and points out that "the relation between background feelings and drives and motivations is intimate: drives express themselves directly as background emotion and we eventually become aware of their existence by means of background feelings...."[16]

Steven Pinker, pyschologist and former director of the Center for Cognitive Neuroscience at the Massachusetts Institute of Technology, writes, "I will show that the emotions are adaptations, well-engineered software modules that work in harmony with the intellect and are indispensable to the functioning of the whole mind."[17] He also claims that

> The emotions are mechanisms that set the brain's highest-level goals. Once triggered by a propitious moment, an emotion triggers a cascade of subgoals and sub-subgoals that we call thinking and acting. Because goals and means are woven into a multipy nested control structure...no sharp line divides thinking from feeling.[18]

Speaking from the standpoint of biology, Edward O. Wilson says, "Emotion is not just a perturbation of reason but a vital part of it."[19] And "without the stimulus and guidance of emotion, rational thought slows and disintegrates."[20]

The Confucian and the evolutionary psychologist thus confirm the fact that, contrary to the traditional Western exclusive prizing of reason in moral deliberation, the emotions are naturally and legitimately involved as well. The emotions love, sympathy, and humaneness underlie the basic sets of Confucian role relations. They underlie the quest for deep knowledge about them and other things (called "embodiment," *tiren*). They lead to such reciprocal actions as filiality and nurturance. Similarly, the modern biologist identifies the emotion of sympathy as motivating altruistic behavior.[21] Robert Trivers says,

> [G]iven the universal and nearly daily practice of reciprocal altruism among humans today, it is reasonable to assume that it has been an important factor in recent human evolution and that the underlying emotional dispositions affecting altruistic behavior have important genetic components.[22]

Shame, for Confucians, is another social emotion that involves both cognition and feeling. It involves knowledge of the rules of conduct (*li*) and knowledge that other people know one has violated them (see the *Analects* citation below). As Daniel Fessler of the University of California at Los Angeles has said, shame motivates conformity. Therefore it fosters cooperative behavior, which is advantageous from an evolutionary point of view. Shame is extremely important as a social control and socialization instrument in Chinese society.

Other biologically based emotions also come into play in reciprocal altruism. Trivers speculates that guilt has been selected in part to deal with someone who has taken a benefit without giving anything back, that is to motivate him to act reciprocally in the future.[23] We can rest assured that cooperative behavior not only functions best when relations are stable and predictable, but also where the human susceptibility to shame and need for peer respect are in operation. Beginning with Mencius, Confucians have had much to offer on the role of these emotions in achieving social control.

BOTH NATURE AND NURTURE

The fourth convergence of positions held by Confucian ethicists and modern biologists concerns how they answer the question: Is human nature malleable? To the Westerner, this topic is one aspect of the old nature versus nurture debate. A distinguished science writer has entitled his book, *Nature Via Nurture*,[24] to indicate that both are involved in each other. This is pretty much the consensus as the new century begins. But why does the old debate endure? Two reasons. One is that to the Westerner, the need to protect free will is a common assumption. Nature is often associated with things we cannot control, that are beyond our choices, nurture with things we can. So some place for nurture will always have its advocates. Free choice is linked to individual responsibility and to deterrence of anti-social acts. The other reason the debate endures is that academic disciplines are divided in the debate. While many disciplines agree that both biology and culture are significantly involved in human social behavior, others tilt to one side. For example, many anthropologists teach that culture (a form of nurture) alone is significant, and there is nothing biological about it. All other influences on behavior are trivialized.

In pre-modern Confucianism, from one perspective, human nature is not changeable. All are born with what Mencius called the "four minds" of compassion, shame, respect, and right and wrong. People may develop these to varying degrees, but the potential to express them is innate to all. The presumption is that even a bad environment cannot cause these to disappear. This perspective is discussed using words about the sameness of people. Yet from another viewpoint, Confucians believed that people are enormously receptive to education. They are perfectible, in the sense that self-cultivation coupled with the acts of teachers and virtuous models can turn around the shabbiest of persons, eliciting his hidden original nature. Hence rather than the blood-line, the favored basis for privilege was the meritocratic civil service examinations (successful education as the criterion of merit) and the state's early interest in establishing schools and controlling curriculum. So, prior to the twentieth century, along with belief in an unchangeable human nature, the idea of malleability coexisted. It was significant in China because it supported the self-fulfilling prophecy that, through education, people can realize their good natures and contribute to a harmonious society. In modern China, this idea energized political reformers, who continued to stress education as a tool of social change, thereby "saving China."

Here again we find one of the many factors that show how some of Confucian ethics is consistent with the actual human condition. The

Mencian portrait combines the confidence in education that goes along with belief in malleability, with the belief that there is also an inborn or fixed basis for some social behavior, in the "four minds." The ultimate foundation of ethics lies not in a supernatural being or realm, but in what the early Confucians called the original mind found in us all at birth, and today we would call biology.

The contemporary scientific position anchors malleability in three domains. The first is the plasticity of the neural pathways in the brain. There are great variations in the pathways used by neurotransmitters, different versions of the same genetic sequence, which allow for different ways in which the pathways interact. This opens the door biologically for vast differences in personalities.[25] Genes also work in teams to produce an organism that flexibly can work in different types of environment.[26] Reference here is to short term malleability that can affect individuals differently. Organisms, such as sponges, are also subject to long term, sometimes continuous, changes in the way they express the genes in their genetic code, that is in how they act and look. Temperature might be the factor causing the change. Such "phenotypic plasticity" is not of interest to those with political agendas.[27] But the malleability of the neural pathways is of interest also, because of the second sense of malleability. It means that educators who convey to students the experience of other humans, can indeed foster the growth of new cortical neurons. Experience, direct or indirect, strengthens neurons that otherwise would atrophy.[28] So the second domain in which malleability is based is the impact of educational experience on the brain. But remember that learning from an educator or from other experience also depends on the genes and the neural circuitry that they help create. Back and forth influences.

There is a third reason for retaining malleability and rejecting total biological determinism in the mix of it with the biologically innate. It is the relative unpredictability of much, but certainly not all, individual human behavior. In part this is because a single nerve cell can get information from many neurons, all subject to alteration by experience.[29] Brain chemistry is constantly impacted by social events. Also, our mind is made up of competing factions.[30] Genes give us selfish motives, and yet also the ability to love and to care for justice. Choice is a fact of human life and is the most proximate, experienced source of our great distance from being only a fixed quantity. Genes often do not operate at all unless signaled to do so by our choices. Natural selection may ease us into behavior that reinforces our reproductive fitness, but we can choose patterns of behavior that go against it, as in the decision to remain childless. Studies of our child-rearing practices and legal system show that people do build into their decisions a sense of the consequences of their actions. We hold individuals responsible, providing they can be aware of the consequences of their decisions to act.[31] Feelings, located in identifiable brain regions, assist us in making choices and help our foresight. Sometimes those feelings are within our control, as we decide which emotionally laden things to allow near us.[32] Books to read and friends with whom to interact are within our control. Mencius realized this.

But contrary to the perspective of some dictators and social scientists who believe "only culture counts," there are limits to our malleability. Our genetic makeup does establish behavior tendencies or patterns or predispositions to certain forms of social behavior. E. O. Wilson would identify such examples as parental investment in offspring, altruism, avoidance of incest, cooperation, and contract making.[33] Others add to the list the quest for esteem and autonomy.[34] In other words, these fixed elements in our natures predispose us (not force us) to make certain choices. This does not deny that predispositions are subject to environmental influence. Nature and nurture are both involved. The predispositions do not determine our conduct. But they are certainly relevant to any description of what we are as humans. The predispositions make it easy for us to perform and build upon certain types of behavior. And they increase the likelihood that social policies that go against the predispositions will fail. Recall the failure of the Maoist communal kitchens and some of the kibbutz communal child rearing practices in Israel. You generally cannot fight family bonds successfully.

NURTURANCE AND IMITATION

The final convergence, concerning nurturance, is an assumption about how people are innately predisposed to learn: through imitation. In China, this topic has been discussed in terms of the presentation of virtuous models for emulation as the most effective way to teach or socialize people. It was said to be effective because it focused on inner transformation, using the self-generated inner control of shame, rather than relying on the outer control of a fear invoking police. As the *Analects* says,

If the people be led by laws, and uniformity sought to be given them by punishments, they will try to avoid the punishment, but have no sense of shame. If they be led by virtue [virtuous models], and uniformity sought to be given them by the rules of propriety, they will have a sense of shame, and moreover will become good.[35]

Here we see the relation of shame (a social emotion) to a knowledge (cognition) of the rules of propriety. Transformed in attitude internally, the person subject to shame will be a good cooperator and survivor.

In contemporary psychology, the term for imitation is "observational learning." Its biological basis involves what are known as "mirror neurons."[36] Mirror neurons enable a person to imitate the movements of others, to read their intentions, mentally to copy their feelings and some of their thinking. It can promote fast learning. And it helps speed the transmission of knowledge and skills within and beyond a society's boundaries. Apprentices copy masters. Empathy, often involved in altruism, depends on cooperation between neural imitation networks and those that regulate emotions, enabling us to mimic the emotions of other people. So our biological predisposition for modeling or observational learning are deeply involved in our ethical life and its nurturance.[37]

CONCLUSION

In the end, the findings of evolutionary biology help us to identify what the strengths and weaknesses are of some fundamentals of Mencian Confucianism. One of these is the power of the predisposition to acts of reciprocal altruism among kin. This lies behind the power of social networks in Chinese society. Many are modeled on the family analogy, though not necessarily involving genetic kin. Especially when legal authorities are weak, they provide protections and services. At the same time, the survival and multiplication and strength of the Chinese people at the group and individual level owe much to the importance of lineages in which the biological principles of kin selection operate. In practice, these often employ the psychology of relationships similar to those in the networks. As a result, there are special feelings and benefits provided to kin. As one biologist puts it,

> [S]election has evidently favored people with the motivational mechanisms, emotional systems, and intellectual capacities that enable us to learn kinship categories, establish links with others, educate others about genealogical relationships, and feel a sense of solidarity and cooperativeness with those identified as relatives, especially with our close relatives.[38]

Mencian Confucians, whether at the philosophical or popular social level would not quarrel with this statement. And much of traditional Chinese education has concerned passing on information about how to organize society with interpersonal rituals that solidify the kinship categories. Another strength is the idea of commitment, found in the Chinese term *zhi*, without which the individual is left only with Mencian and evolutionary descriptions of human tendencies to love, sympathy, and reciprocal altruism. Its importance has only recently been noted among some evolutionary psychologists.[39]

There remains a serious weakness in a society and ethic with such pronounced concerns with kinship categories. From the biologists standpoint, a Confucian weakness is not taking account of the fact that in-group out-group distinctions are also genetically based. Aggressive behavior is common between them. The tribal instinct coexists with the altruistic. Our natures are not one-dimensional. Biologists have argued that both have proven useful over time. Patriotism, based on the tribal, is necessary when one's society is threatened. Even in pursuit of the aims of patriotism, cooperation involving reciprocity with allies, may also be essential. The big question is how to deal with the conflict between the altruistic and the out-group perspectives. Do these facts mean that a modern version of Mencian ethics must be revised to indicate that human nature is multi-dimensional? Yes, they do. Such in-group/out-group boundaries also obstruct the flow of information that obstructs good problem solving and the growth of new knowledge. The boundaries limit the number of people and variety of perspectives brought to bear on an issue. They foster cronyism and corruption. The actual limits for the altruism of even the most highly educated Confucian civil servant was probably the county in which he might serve as a magistrate. Here is where laws, national and international, are so important, to promote equality before the law, especially for people outside of our networks. Here is an important contribution of Western culture to repairing the failure of Mencian ethics to deal practically with altruism beyond the family. Only the law, the oversight agencies that help enforce its intent, and popular attitudes that respect both laws and agencies, are a practical solution to the problem of duty beyond the boundaries of kin and community.

5

Mencius and an Ethics of the New Century

I have never met anyone who tried to use either the ethics of Plato's *Republic* or the Epicurean hedonism of Lucretius' *On the Nature of Things* as a guide for living. So I would not spend time asking if there was any compatibility between either of them, on the one hand, and some serious contemporary Western ethics, on the other. But I have met Chinese people who treat the *Mencius* as such a guide. I think that Arthur Danto was on target when he made these comments about some non-Western literature:

> The difficulty with our approach to non-Western literature is that it fails to adequately address the issue of these texts' Otherness. I am not arguing for relativism of any sort. But in non-Western cultures there are values other than truth and ways of addressing books other than by analyzing their content. For texts are things that have to be lived, as many books of the Orient are lived—their vitality as writing bound up with their being vitally a part of the lives of their readers in a way that they cannot be with ours.[1]

I expect that some people will continue to treat the *Mencius* as a text to be lived, well into the twenty-first century. Every age picks and chooses which parts of a complicated text it wishes to emphasize. Therefore, I ask myself how much ethical theory from within the *Mencius* do I believe will endure in the new century, in China or in other societies that may treat the Chinese texts attentively. My answer is that those aspects that are compatible with evolutionary biology will survive a sifting to become for the new century the essence of the *Mencius* text, separated from what will then be disregarded as the dross.

---

* First published in Alan K. L. Chan ed., *Mencius: Contexts and Interpretations* (Honolulu: University of Hawaii Press, 2002), pp. 305–315.

A Darwinian perspective dominates contemporary human biology and psychology, perspectives respectively identified as sociobiology and as evolutionary psychology. This means that both accept the principle that human behavior reflects the reciprocal impact of genes and culture. Those genes that dominate in large groups (not necessarily individuals) do so because they increase the likelihood that the people will be more fit for survival and for reproducing their genes. The psychologists refer to the genetic roots as "hard-wiring." They say that hard-wired within our brains are hereditary rules for mental development, for viewing the world in a certain way, and for making certain choices. Some sociobiologists call these rules epigenetic. I assume that such principles will dominate biology and psychology well into the next century. I also assume that any ethical position that expects to be treated seriously during this time by people who accept the Darwinian trends must have essential tenets that are compatible with those principles, as fleshed out.

Edward O. Wilson is the most prominent spokesman for the sociobiological position, and so I will take his positions on relevant issues as representative. He gets off to a start that is promising to anyone who wishes to treat Mencian ethics with respect. That is, he accepts the premise that there is a human nature, a concept for which Mencius is well known. Wilson defines it as the hereditary rules for mental development that bias cultural evolution.[2] This is an age in which many scholars in the humanities and in anthropology/sociology are so focused on the differences between people and on the uniqueness of individual cultures that they condemn belief in a human nature as "essentialism." Some call this anti-essentialist perspective postmodern. But even the anti-postmodernist American philosopher Richard Rorty (*Truth and Progress*) says that we should stop asking what our nature is and instead ask "What can we make of ourselves?".[3] In short, Rorty also opposes use of the expression "human nature." This is a curious position that reveals Rorty as both opposed to foundationalist ethics (where ethics would be based on human nature) and as also an acknowledged Darwinian.

The belief in a common human nature does not require belief that, correcting for environmental variations, all people's minds are the same. Describing the findings of the brain scientist Dr. Gerald Edelman, one writer says,

> Thus, every person, even an identical twin, has a network of connections within his or her brain different from that in every other brain. Every

person's individual network has been shaped by Darwinian rules of selection to provide a structure that will enable him or her to cope with the world.[4]

A COMMON HUMAN NATURE

Mencian ethics in the new century has an optimistic starting point. The biologists and psychologists to whom I referred would have no trouble with the Mencian assumption that there is a common human nature. This is important because it affirms that ethics can be grounded in the innate human condition. In other words, certain moral concepts derive from something that is inborn. They are not entirely arbitrary human inventions relative to individual communities and cultures. Whether or not they are also founded on something transcendental is another question. For now, I begin with a general description of the theory about an innate nature from which the moral concepts derive. Then I will take up its content.

In simple terms, the contemporary Darwinian and Mencian theories share the position that ethical rules derive from biology, that is from our hereditary or inborn human nature. Just below I give an example of Mencius' use of an empirical argument on this matter. The *Mencius* also implies that human nature is in turn derived from Heaven, "... a man who knows his own nature will know heaven."[5] This claim has no Darwinian counterpart. It would be rejected today by many biologists and psychologists, along with similar claims that base ethics on God's commands.

There is no necessary connection between a biological claim (a testable claim about an innate response) and a religious claim (not testable). Mencius gives various examples of the innate traits that he affirms exist[6] and of the religious kind of claims.[7] This means that someone today can filter the Heaven out of Mencius (the religious claims) and still retain a justification for much of his ethics. So the biological basis of ethics is the first Mencian position that is likely to endure.

This basis is important as a rule of thumb for sorting through the barrage of varying ethical rules that a person may encounter today. Only those consistent with human nature will survive in the long term.[8] Those that are inconsistent, such as Shaker celibacy, will have short lives. To affirm a biological basis is to affirm the existence of transcultural moral instincts, such as territoriality and the incest taboo. Of course there are exceptions to the practice of these instincts, but they are sufficiently limited in scope so as not to contradict the basic principles of survival and reproductive success.

ITS EMPIRICAL BASIS

There is a general point I would make about the enduring vibrancy of the Mencian theory of human nature. Certain parts of it can last because they are compatible with the standard of empirical testing. This is the case with one of the most famous arguments Mencius presents, namely the automatic response of an observer to seeing a child in danger of falling into a well. Mencius predicts immediate acts to save the child, devoid of any cost-benefit calculation.[9] He treats this as evidence of the existence of the moral instinct of empathy for suffering and altruistic response to do something about it. In principle, a person could set up an experiment involving children teetering on wells and see if neutral observers would so act. He is arguing that we both can (a matter that we call biological and Mencius would call an inborn heart) and should act with compassion. This is the point.

Belief in innate moral sentiments is quite compatible with evidence that under extreme conditions they can also be non existent in people who previously exhibited them. Auschwitz survivor Primo Levi wrote

> In conclusion: theft in Buna, punished by the civil direction, is authorized and encouraged by the SS; is considered by the civilians as a normal exchange operation; theft among Haftlinge is generally punished, but the punishment strikes the thief and the victim with equal gravity. We now invite the reader to contemplate the possible meaning in the Lager of the words 'good' and 'evil', 'just' and 'unjust'.[10]

But the moral sentiments of those same persons could return. Levi wrote of the offer of a slice of bread by some inmates to others who had been working, shortly after the SS guards had fled:

> Only a day before a similar event would have been inconceivable. The law of the Lager said: 'eat your own bread, and if you can, that of your neighbor', and left no room for gratitude [for the offer of bread]. It [the offer of bread] really meant the Lager was dead.

> It was the first human gesture that occurred among us. I believe that that moment can be dated as the beginning of the change by which we who had not died slowly changed from Haftlinge to men again.[11]

So the empirical argument for certain innate moral sentiments can withstand this counterexample. It does need updating, namely acknowledgment that they may evaporate under certain circumstances.

To return to his form of argument, in fact, Mencius uses many different types of argument at various places in the text. Sometimes he argues from analogy, a technique widespread in different cultures, including our own. For example, he approves of the plant analogy to explain the potentiality of our innate moral instincts.[12] He says that his interpretation of the water analogy to explain human nature is superior to that of his debating partner, Gaozi.[13] A second type is the argument from behavioral implications. If people accept a given position, it is psychologically likely to affect their behavior in a certain positive or negative way. For example, he argues against Gaozi that if people believe that behaving dutifully is artificial or not natural to the human condition, they will not be motivated to do the right thing: "If you must mutilate the willow [by analogy, human nature] to make it into cups and bowls [to generate moral conduct], must you mutilate a man to make him moral? Surely it will be these words of yours men in the world will follow in bringing disaster upon morality."[14] There are arguments from authority, such as the practices of the sage kings Yao and Shun.[15] And there are arguments from utility. These may include the utility of providing models to the people, for then they will follow the model: "If there is one who is not [fond of killing people], then the people of the Empire will crane their necks to watch for his coming. this being truly the case, the people will turn to him like water flowing downwards with a tremendous force."[16] Or, they may include the utility of policies, such as tax reduction, for improving the lives of the people. While acknowledging the existence of many forms of argument, I point to the explicit existence of those from empirical evidence to show the compatibility of Mencius with the standards of verification likely to dominate in our new century.

Actually, Mencius uses the argument from analogy to bolster his empirical argument for universal traits and for universal standards. His child and the well argument goes from establishing the existence of a trait of spontaneous compassion to treating compassion as a universal duty. Mencius would have us infer from a universal trait of human nature to a universal standard. For him, as for Xunzi, the analogy of carpentry tools conveyed the abstraction that Westerners call a universal. These are the various carpentry tools that give the same result no matter where or when they are used: the plumb line, the balance scale, the compass, and the square. Giving the same results universally, they also provide a standard. By analogy, the sage, whose nature we share, also is a universal standard of human perfection. Mencius said, "The compass and the carpenter's square are the culmination of squares and circles; the sage is the culmination of humanity."[17] The argument is that we know perfection exists from the carpenter's tools. By analogy, we know there are degrees of perfection in human nature, with the sage as the highest degree. To repeat, the existence of a common human nature is assumed.

The strength of the Mencian positions thus far include his belief in a common human nature and his use of the empirical argument. In addition, he will have three other theses that are positive from the standpoint of the ethics of the new century. One is the identification of what is innate and of primary moral significance as an emotion. The second is that the primal emotion is kinship love, on the basis of which empathy is learned. Bringing him up to date, I would suggest that the Mencian refer to "caregiver" rather than kin, because in fact persons other than kin enter into the familial roles. The third is his characterization of the mind as an evaluative process.

EMOTIONS AND DELIBERATION

To identify the content of the theories of human nature shared by Mencius and modern Darwinians reveals something that sets Confucian ethics apart from most previous Western ethical systems.

This is the prominence of the emotions in Mencian moral deliberations and its relative absence in prominent Western systems. From the nineteenth century onward, Kantianism and utilitarianism have dominated Western ethics. In the former case, reasoning about the applicability of the categorical imperative dominates consideration of action choices. In the latter, it is cost-benefit calculations about the greatest happiness for the greatest number of persons. In both cases, the thinking is supposedly rational, devoid of much emotion. In contrast, Mencius places the emotions of compassion and shame at the center of his moral psychology. He also says that our sense of duty (*yi*) pleases the heart just as meat pleases the taste buds.[18] In other words, we find the emotion of joy joined with the cognitive sense that something is a duty.

Similarly, E. O. Wilson affirms that "[Brain scientists] have established that passion is inseverably linked to reason. Emotion is not just a perturbation of reason but a vital part of it."[19] And, "Without the stimulus and guidance of emotion, rational thought slows and dis-integrates."[20] Among other things, this means that the emotions provide the motivation that leads to action. In treating compassion and shame as among the root moral sentiments, Mencius was focusing on emotions that are basic to doing the right thing. E. O. Wilson agrees with the basic Mencian assumption that "moral concepts are derived from innate emotions."[21]

INFANT BONDING AND SYMPATHY

Infant bonding with caregivers and sympathy are among the specific emotions that are central to the innate emotions singled out by both Mencius and the Darwinians. E. O. Wilson writes: "Among traits with documented heritability, those closest to moral aptitude are empathy with the distress of others and certain processes of attachment between infants and their caregivers."[22] Obviously, there will be considerable difference in the specifics of what the emotions involve. Mencius will focus on patriarchal emotions, such as those between father and son,[23] though such a relationship is absent from Wilson's work. The important point is the connection that both parties see between kinship and sympathy or altruism. Mencius says that the gentleman first treats his kin as kin, and then treats the people with humaneness.[24] Also, "Loving one's kin [especially parents] is humaneness."[25] Among the hereditary rules of mental development making up E. O. Wilson's concept of human nature are the details of mother-infant bonding.[26] "Kin selection [involving the natural selection of genes and their effect on genetic relatives] is especially important in the origin of altruistic behavior."[27] Altruism is an emotion.[28]

James Q. Wilson is a social scientist who draws heavily on evolutionary theory, genetics, brain science, and primatology. He also takes his evidence from anthropology, psychology, and education. Like Mencius he believes in an innate moral sense. Like Mencius, he finds that sympathy is rooted in kinship emotions: "For most children the ability to be affected by the emotional state of others leads to a concern for the well-being of others."[29] Again, this is a matter of an emotion. He says, "Much of the time our inclination toward fair play or our sympathy for the plight of others are immediate and instinctive, a reflex of our emotions more than an act of our intellect, and in those cases in which we do deliberate ... our deliberations begin ... with feelings—in short, with a moral sense."[30] This moral sense is nearly universal.[31] In short, it is part of human nature. The two Wilsons do not always agree. James Q. would reject the claim of E. O. that investment in child care is driven only by a desire to reproduce one's genes.[32] But they both follow the 1906 finding of Edward Westermarck the "the maternal sentiment is universal in mankind."[33]

THE EVALUATING MIND

James Q. Wilson also argues for another aspect of the content of human nature favored by Mencius. When Mencius refers to the *shifei zhi xin* or the mind of right and wrong, he is claiming that humans evaluate. The human mind is an evaluating mind. Wilson says that one meaning of the claim that there is an innate moral sense is that "virtually everyone, beginning at a very young age, makes moral judgments that, though they may vary greatly in complexity, sophistication, and wisdom, distinguish between actions on the grounds that some are right and others wrong...."[34] There is a sign that we differentiate between matters of taste and matters that carry moral praise or blame. This sign is the general feeling that if we are going to violate a standard based on a common moral impulse, we must give justifications.

Both Wilsons agree on the existence of a moral sense. E. O. Wilson says,

> Such a process [leading to the predominance of genes predisposing people toward cooperative behavior] repeated through thousands of generations inevitably gave birth to the moral sentiments. With the exception of stone psychopaths (if any truly exist), these instincts are vividly experienced by every person variously as conscience, self-respect, remorse, empathy, shame, humility, and moral outrage.[35]

EMPATHY AND THE OUT-GROUP: THE MENCIAN GAP

Some people may not care about the child at the well and do nothing. They may even throw the child in the well. One piece of Holocaust literature can represent the countless documented instances of Nazi barbarity towards children. This is from Elie Wiesel's Memoirs.

> Unable to 'handle' such a large number of Hungarian Jews in the crematoria, the killers were not content merely to incinerate children's dead bodies. In

their barbarous madness they cast living Jewish children into specially tended furnaces.

... I see them now, and I still curse the killers, their accomplices, the indifferent spectators who knew and kept silent ...[36]

Obviously, this kind of episode exhibits the existence of in-group/out-group behavior. If any group expressed it starkly, the Nazis did, and their Ukrainian guards as well. Sociobiologists base this behavior in an instinct. They would say that the instinct to differentiate in-group from out-group and to favor the former can coexist with the instincts of empathy and altruism. Sociobiologists call it a tribal instinct, but "tribal" is not in favor with anthropologists these days, except when referring to some places such as India. They generally prefer the term "ethnic group." In any case, the Darwinians would insist that there are innate dispositions to divide people into in-group and out-group categories. Such sentiments will periodically be in conflict with empathy and altruism. Our natures are not one dimensional. The tribal instinct coexists with the altruistic. I suspect that both have proven useful over time. The tribal is probably the basis of the value of patriotism that is especially necessary when one's society is threatened. At other times, there are broad benefits to altruism. The big question is how we deal with the conflict between the altruistic and the out-group perspectives.

So Mencius is on solid ground in affirming that our ethics rests heavily on common human emotions associated with caregivers, on his insight that sympathy grows from those emotions, on noting that our mind is an evaluating mind, and on seeing the emotional dimension of moral choice rather than treating it as exclusively cognitive. However, from a contemporary perspective, his weakness is in not dealing with in-group/out-group distinctions that limit the scope of our empathy. The solution for the modern Mencian is to study the question of the possible survival value of enlarging group cooperation. Biologists have already done some work on this matter. E. O. Wilson says that there is empirical evidence that "cooperative individuals generally survive longer and leave more offspring."[37] There are seeds, but only seeds, in the Mencius for developing that idea. They lie in the opposition to Yang Zhu egoism and in the argument that productive role divisions and cooperation in the exchange of output are in the interest of people as a whole. Farmers and craftsmen trade grain for implements: "Moreover, it is necessary for each man to use the products of all the hundred crafts."[38]

How one realizes this activity is another matter. It requires both the rule of law and stable institutions, both matters neglected by Mencius. Respect for cooperation as a value can also be taught. With their highly developed educational concerns, we might hope that the modern followers of Mencius would have something to contribute here.

6

A Modern Way to Justify Ethical Rules: J. S. Mill, Mencius, and Current Biology

A central question in ethics is: How can we justify ethical rules or moral choices? Many ways have been tried, some similar in both China and the United States. One of these ways is both consistent with contemporary biology and also meets the test of producing action. That is, it motivates people to do what they think is right. This way is to justify the values that form our standard by showing that human nature is so constituted from birth that we prefer certain objects. Rules and choices are then legitimate to the degree that they promote or obstruct attaining those objects. This is also the approach of Mill and Mencius.

Among the other, competing candidates for ways to justify rules, popular at some time in China and the United States, one is the assertion that the moral rules are commands of an external, transcendental Being. Such commands require the duty of obedience, backed up by rewards and punishments. In the Judeo-Christian tradition, the Being is God, and the commands are most simply summed up in the Ten Commandments, the first four of which require commitment to a particular religious doctrine. The individual has the free will that enables him to choose to obey or disobey, and he has the responsibility to obey. He is subject to praise or blame for choosing rightly or wrongly. In China, the Being would be a Heaven that also issues commands. This view of Heaven existed in the Western Zhou and in the thought of Dong Zhongshu (179?–104? B.C.).

---

* Slightly modified from the first English version, published in James St. Andre ed., *Hanxue zongheng* (Excursions in Sinology) (Hong Kong: Shangwu yinshuguan, 2002), pp. 180–194, and from the Chinese version published as "Yi zhong zhengming lunli guize di xiandai fangshi," in Harvard-Yenching Institute and Sanlian shudian eds., *Rujia yu ziyouzhuyi* (Confucianism and liberalism) (Beijing: Sanlian shudian, 2001), pp. 201–212.

Some, not all, Confucians treated Heaven as transcendental. Mencius did not. And although his text does say that "a man who knows his own nature will know Heaven,"[1] Heaven does not play a significant role in the grounding of his ethics.

Another candidate is ethical relativism. This position maintains that ethical rules are statements of what people (or elders) in a specific society say is right and wrong or good and bad. The sanctions to obey them come from peers or authorities in that society. And the rules vary from one cultural group to another. At their basis is the principle of cultural relativism, nicely formulated in the United States by the late anthropologist Melville Herskovits: "Judgments are based on experience, and experience is interpreted by each individual in terms of his own enculturation."[2] Ethical judgments are included in the category of what is formed by enculturation. In China the most famous ethical relativists were disciples of Zhuangzi (369?–286?). Parts of the External and Miscellaneous sections of the text that bears his name, make a powerful case that each school of thought has its own perspective, especially on ethical matters, and so each sees only a portion of the *dao*. The "Autumn Floods" chapter contains many examples.

I follow what the biologist Edward O. Wilson calls the empiricist position.[3] Others call it the naturalistic view. Because this approach will anchor ethical rules in human nature and a related ethical position, its advocates today must begin by challenging those who would deny the very existence of such a thing as human nature. Those opponents include disciples of one of the founders of modern anthropology, Franz Boas, as well as many contemporary anthropologists, whose perspective motivates them to stress the uniqueness of each society and its people. Mao Zedong is another recent enemy of the concept. He writes, "Is there such a thing as human nature? Of course there is. But there is only human nature in the concrete, no human nature in the abstract. In a class society, there is only human nature that bears the stamp of a class; human nature that transcends classes does not exist."[4] Even the American philosopher Richard Rorty objects to the concept.[5]

The task for the biologist, then, is to identify the content of this human nature. They say that it is the mind, which consists of genetically specialized neural networks ("modules") that evolve over time, according to regular patterns of development. An example is the language instinct that applies grammar to sounds or words. Such networks also underlie sympathy for others and forethought (often central to pleasure and pain), which involve information processing and emotions. This evolving over time can be heavily influenced by experience, and, in some cases, modules can change location in the brain. The modules are products of genes that endure because they promote survival or their own reproduction in subsequent generations. These patterns make it likely that all humans, excepting the brain damaged, will, in some regards, feel, think, act, and experience needs in predictable ways. This is especially true of certain types of thinking and acting. My own position on human nature is influenced by these biologists. However, because it focuses on the implications of the position for ethics, it singles out two of the patterns of thinking, acting, feeling, and needing that I consider most relevant to ethics. One has its pre-modern ancestor in the utilitarianism of Jeremy Bentham and J. S. Mill, and the other in the Confucianism of Mencius. Thus my position is definitely not identical to that of those biologists. If anything, it is inspired by the psychologist Steven Pinker's recognition that discoveries about human nature must be combined with statements about our value systems. In my case, that value system is a modified utilitarianism, accepting two premises of classical utilitarianism and rejecting a third.

The empiricist as ethicist will anchor certain ethical precepts and associated emotions in a universal human nature that is accessible to biological study. Human nature is where those brain modules, manifest as two patterns, reside. I will now identify what the patterns of interest to me are.

The first is an aversion to suffering or pain, and a receptivity to pleasure or happiness. Ever since the Epicureans in classical Greece and Rome, pain and pleasure have included mental stress and tranquility as well as the consequences of damage to living tissue and chemical imbalance. The neurologist Antonio Damasio says that "Pain is the consequence of a state of local dysfunction in a living tissue, the consequence of a state of a stimulus—impending or actual tissue damage—which causes the sensation of pain...."[6] He also distinguishes pain sensation from the individual's consciousness of that dysfunction, which he calls "pain affect." In contrast he says that "Pleasure, on the other hand, is all about forethought. It is related to the clever anticipation of what can be done not to have a problem ."[7] The problem may be some imbalance, for example low blood sugar, experienced as hunger or thirst. Pleasure then arises in the process of seeking food or drink.

Following Jeremy Bentham, J. S. Mill identifies the universal human interest in avoiding pain and in seeking happiness and made it the basis of his utilitarianism. It is still a powerful position in the United States. The science writer Robert Wright explores the new science of evolutionary psychology in his book, *The Moral Animal.*[8] He writes, "Belief in the goodness of happiness and the badness of suffering isn't just a basic part of moral discourse that we all share. Increasingly it seems to be the only basic part that we all share."[9] Like Mill, his premise is that everyone accepts the utilitarian mandate to apply this rule: right and wrong are a function of the pain/happiness consequences, if people always do a certain thing. Utilitarianism provides a basis for humanitarian action. I include myself in that "everyone" who accepts this mandate. The Australian philosopher Peter Singer is another advocate.[10] The utilitarians also accept the principle that each person is the best judge of his or her interests, where happiness is concerned. Mill adds that education can rectify inadequacies of the judgment of some people. In any case, especially with Bentham, there is an assumption of natural equality of ability on this matter of judging interest.[11]

Bentham, Mill, and Singer also all accept the principle that in calculating the cost/ benefit consequences of deeds, "each [person is] to count for one and none for more than one." This produces an equality of right. Eventually, in his middle years, Bentham based his advocacy of representative democracy on these principles of equality.

I can accept the utilitarian mandate, and the idea that each person is the best judge of his own interest (plus the related belief in representative democracy). However, I depart from them in their third premise, the insistence that no one person's happiness counts for more than any other person's. I reject the view that, when I am the agent, all other people share an equality of right, that is, an equal claim on my concern. This is where the Chinese legacy from Mencius, brought up to date with the findings of modern evolutionary biology, must be added as a second, biologically based, pattern in our thought and action.

The weakness of the utilitarian position on each person counting for one is that it does not take account of the gradations of emotional attachment that we have to people, based on kinship ties. We can have humanitarian obligations while also acting preferentially toward kin. Long ago the Confucians recognized that the humane or benevolent sentiments (*ren*) which people feel and act on are rooted in those family ties. The *Analects* notes that filiality to parents and proper behavior toward elder brothers is the root of *ren.*[12] The *Mencius* adds that "loving one's parents is benevolence [*ren*]."[13] In discussing what he claims is the innate human aversion to seeing suffering, he says that the way to be able to act according to that sentiment is to begin with the family and work outward. "Treat the aged of your own family in a manner befitting their venerable age and extend this treatment to the aged of other families; treat your own young in a manner befitting their tender age and extend this to the young of other families, and you can roll the Empire in your palm."[14] The early etymological dictionary, *Shuowen* says that *ren* is love, meaning kinship love.

All kinds of differences separate Mencian Confucians from the modern biologists. For example, the latter find altruism beginning in the behavior of elders to younger kin (sometimes the reverse of the patriarchal Confucian position); the subject for the biologist is genes rather than occupants of social roles (such as father-son), and Confucian references to universal traits probably contain a pro male gender bias. But the Mencian Confucian and the biologist still share a very basic position: altruism begins in the family and spreads outward. Edward O. Wilson says,

> *Kin selection* is the natural selection of genes based on their effects on individuals carrying them plus the effects the presence of the genes has on all the genetic relatives of the individuals, including parents, children, siblings, cousins, and others who still live and are capable either of reproducing or of affecting the reproduction of blood relatives. Kin selection is especially important in the origin of altruistic behavior.[15]

The seminal work on altruism was done by Robert Trivers in 1971, building on 1964 work of William D. Hamilton. Trivers states that "The preconditions for the evolution of reciprocal altruism are similar to those for the operation of kin selection...."[16] And Robert Wright describes the outward spread of the altruism like this: "A gene that repaid kindness with kindness could thus have spread through the extended family, and, by interbreeding, to other families, where it would thrive on the same logic."[17] Reciprocal altruism then can be preserved as the value of cooperation, which bridges genetically unrelated people, because it is beneficial to both parties. Trivers sees this confirmed in the studies on the Prisoner's Dilemma of the game theorist Anatole Rappaport.[18] Robert Wright describes additional tests of the tendency toward reciprocity in the work of Robert Axelrod, which underscore the fact that sharing information is crucial to successful cooperation, leading to a win-win result. And Matt Ridley notes that the principal condition required for the reciprocating of kind acts is "a stable, repetitive relationship."[19] This is the kind of relationship in which people come to know each other's likely behavior. It is epitomized in Confucian role relationships. Wilson writes, "To the heritability of moral aptitude add the abundant evidence of history that cooperative individuals generally survive longer and leave more offspring."[20]

I am not the first person to criticize classical utilitarianism for its ignoring of the individual's emotions and attachments in calculating happiness consequences. Bernard Williams has noted that, by doing so, utilitarianism can cause an alienation from morality itself.[21] The inner feelings of humans have been ignored by Western ethicists in favor of a primary focus on obligation and blame. Wilson says, "Without the stimulus and guidance of emotion, rational thought slows and disintegrates."[22] People generally do have special emotions for family members. A moral choice that ignores them may be one that fosters alienation from morality. I legitimately treat each of my kin as counting for more than one unit of those impacted by my choice in the allocation of my resources and caring. The emotions involved in family bonds are among the emotions that motivate action. This claim that our reasons for acting involve subjective feelings or emotions is not simply an assumption, as H. L. A. Hart maintains.[23] It is a common finding of neurologists,[24] biologists,[25] and psychologists. Steven Pinker, former member of the Center for Cognitive Neuroscience at M.I.T., writes, "The emotions are mechanisms that set the brain's highest-level goals.... No sharp line divides thinking from feeling...."[26]

The emotional bonds to close kin are not the only ones important in ethics. Robert Trivers identifies these others as also genetically based and underlying reciprocal altruism: liking and disliking (found in friendship), indignation (at non altruists), sympathy, and guilt (which may motivate a cheater, one who takes from the altruist but does not reciprocate, to compensate for his misdeeds).[27]

"Each to count for one and none for more than one." If anyone is looking for evidence that this is an impractical rule because it ignores our special preferences for kin, he need only look at the last few lines of a profile of Peter Singer in *The New Yorker* magazine. Tragically, his mother fell ill with Alzheimer's disease, and he was spending a great deal of money on her private care. When asked how he squares this with his position that we should do what is morally right without regard for family relations, he replied, "Perhaps it is more difficult than I thought before, because it is different when it's your mother."[28]

So I find it necessary to appeal to two empirically based universals of human nature to justify ethical rules and choices. First, my ethical standard is a modified utilitarianism. It recognizes our shared human interest in avoiding pain and maximizing happiness and approves of it. This motivates me to care what happens to some people outside of my family and others with whom I have similar bonds. It justifies support for some humanitarian action. But there is also reciprocal altruism, which reveals something of my natural priorities, while also opening the door to altruism beyond kin. A bird that gives a warning call alerts other birds at the cost of revealing its own location to a predator. But in the long run, its genetic kin will benefit, as will some other birds, and some of them will most likely one day return the favor. Studies of reciprocal altruism among birds, fish, and humans, coupled with the work on game theory give me additional reason to be cooperative with non kin rather than selfish. It is consistent with our genetic make-up, and it works. The weakest statement I can make about these facts of human nature is that "they are relevant" to my ethical choices. Like a good Confucian, I will give special consideration to my family members in the allocation of my resources and care. I will take comfort in the fact that any ethic that ignores these bonds is impractical and may turn people away from thinking about the moral variables in choice. However, this does not stop me from also being altruistic to those outside my family.

Needless to say, the claims of other people on my resources and care may conflict with my own individual calculation of what their interest is. There is no way to avoid living with values that sometimes conflict. In this case the competing values would be, either preserving equality of wisdom in ethical judgments (adding in Mill's educational supplement), or the value of special preference for family. This is where law comes in, to try to balance the contesting claims. Specifically, it is the realm of laws and rules dealing with conflict of interest, between, on the one hand, the individual with decision making power and his family, and, on the other, the interest of other people affected by such decisions. In principle, it should protect others against me if I want to grab too much for my own family. In practice, it often falls short. This can occur when popular attitudes of respect for law are weak.

There are several advantages to the human nature based position that I have described in the justification of ethical rules and choices. One is that its claims are testable over time, either in the biological laboratories or in the activities of game theorists such as Robert Axelrod. Another is that it provides factual evidence to reject the influential Platonic view of the mind in which the faculties of the mind are separated; people were encouraged to separate emotions from knowing, because the emotions have been considered a bodily distraction to reason. Instead, the empiricist sees the emotions as assisting the organism to maintain life. Third, the position I have presented is practical. An ethic that is inconsistent with human nature will not, in the long run, work. It will disappear, along with Shaker celibacy.

Finally, it is compatible with what we need in a doctrine of free will, in order to get on with the business of life. This is because there is a difference between crude biological determinism and the position of the evolutionary psychologist. The former does not recognize that there is a difference between my goals and my gene's goals.[29] My genes may make it very pleasant to have sex and produce children. But, due to cultural influences, I may choose not to do either, or only to have sex. As Steven Pinker noted, if my genes don't like it, they can go to the devil. Further, there are always competing motives in my mind (aggression *and* cooperation, breaking a noisy neighbor's window *and* showing my respect for the law). We have innate motives that lead to good deeds and to evil deeds. In the long run, the patterns of human choice are somewhat predictable. But, as purposive beings, our human choices are, in the short run, often unpredictable.[30] This does not prove indeterminism, but it denies support to those who would reject free will. To believe that every choice has a cause, biological or cultural, is also not the same as fatalism. The empiricist who falls overboard from a ship will still call out for help, where the fatalist will not bother. The former thinks his call will have an impact on the choices of the crew on the ship. Finally, the hard headed biological determinist still needs the hypothesis of free will to justify the practicality of blaming criminals and children who are being socialized. But he must also believe in the causative effect of blaming on the choices of others, if he thinks the blaming will change their behavior. So what we end with is, once again, the untidy mixture that is life: we keep the idea of freedom because it works, and we subvert its traditional content by also agreeing that every choice has a cause, cultural, social, biological, or all of the above.

In the West, prior to Darwin, the issue of justifying moral rules had a somewhat different focus from what it had in China. That Western focus was more on arguing for free will than on finding a plausible psychological portrait of human nature, as it was in Confucianism. The reason is that the idea of human free will was necessary in order to clear an omnipotent and good God (the source of those rules) of responsibility for evil. Blame would lie instead with the individual who abuses free choice about whether to obey those rules. This Judeo-Christian theological baggage is absent in China. In orthodox Neo-Confucianism, evil is simply part of the way the physical world is. The major concern of Zhu Xi (1130–1200) was not assigning blame for bad deeds but learning how to remove obstructions to clear thinking that made those deeds happen. There was discussion of choice, but much more discussion on the psychological basis of ethics in human nature. So there is reason to think that modern Chinese will find the new biology congenial to their ethical concerns. They will be less worried than some Westerners have been that apparent biological determinism is muddying the doctrine of free will, thereby removing the grounding of morality (that they feel must include obligation to obey God's rules, responsibility for doing so, and justified blaming if the person fails to do so). Morality can still be grounded, in a sound portrait of human nature. Arguments for belief in free will can still be sound, even if disconnected from the Judeo-Christian theology.

May, 2000

7

Human Malleability and
Its Contexts

There are lots of ways to talk about human plasticity, but few topics have been more quick to ignite a violent debate in modern times, whether in China or in the West. The quality of debate depends on the meaning of malleability at hand, and on the ethical or political implications that participants read into it. The only thing about which one can assume consensus is that the subject of the discussion is socially non trivial traits. Are these universal and fixed, or can they be chosen by the individual or culturally molded? It is agreed that trivial traits vary, are not universal. Obviously, some people are tall and others short.

To the Westerner, this topic is one aspect of the old nature versus nurture debate. A popular science writer has entitled his book, *Nature Via Nurture*,[1] to indicate that both are involved in each other. This is pretty much the consensus as the new century begins. But why does the old debate endure? Two reasons. One is that to the Westerner, the need to protect free will is a common assumption. Nature is often associated with things we cannot control, that are beyond our choices, nurture with things we can. So some place for nurture will always have its advocates. Free choice is linked to individual responsibility and to deterrence of anti-social acts. More on the free will issue below. The other reason is that academic disciplines are divided in the debate. While many disciplines agree that both biology and culture are significantly involved in human social behavior, others tilt to one side. For example, many anthropologists teach that culture (a form of nurture) alone is significant, and there is nothing biological about it. All other influences on behavior are trivialized.

In pre-modern Confucianism, from one perspective, human nature is not changeable. All are born with what Mencius called the "four minds" of compassion, shame, respect, and right and wrong. People may develop these to varying degrees, but the potential to express them is innate to all. The presumption is that even a bad environment cannot cause these to disappear. This perspective is discussed using words about the sameness of people. Yet from another viewpoint, Confucians believed that people are enormously receptive to education. They are perfectible, in the sense that self-cultivation coupled with the acts of teachers and virtuous models can turn around the shabbiest of persons, eliciting his hidden original nature. Hence rather than the blood-line, the favored basis for privilege was the meritocratic civil service examinations (successful education as the criterion of merit) and the state's early interest in establishing schools and controlling curriculum. So, prior to the twentieth century, along with belief in an unchangeable human nature, the idea of malleability coexisted. It was significant in China because it supported the self-fulfilling prophecy that, through education, people can realize their good natures and contribute to a harmonious society. In modern China, this idea energized political reformers, who continued to stress education as a tool of social change, thereby "saving China."

During the years that Maoism dominated Chinese intellectual life (1949–1976), malleability again was front and center. The way in which it was explained in China at that time reflected political considerations of a kind found in England and the United States, when the topic appeared in the sociobiology debates of the last three decades of the last century. So the first part of this brief essay shows how there are trans-cultural, not simply Chinese, dimensions to the topic. The last part of the essay summarizes the emerging consensus of scientific opinion on plasticity that has tried to distance itself from the political quarrel.

MALLEABILITY TRUMPS THE INNATE NATURE

Among the hated Confucian legacies to which Mao attributed some of China's weakness, the Mencian idea of a fixed and universal human nature stands out. To Mao, claims about an innate nature fail on two points. One is that the idea of universality ignores the class differences that divide people by differences in their social natures; difference trumps "four mind" commonality. The other is that innate suggests unchangeable. Psychologically, that suggests that people cannot be changed so as to become the instrument of rapidly changing China socially and eco-nomically. So China cannot be saved, and there is no glorious role for leaders as the teachers of the people in seeking the salvation. In the three fields most accessible to control by its cultural and propaganda agents, the idea of human malleability carried the day: philosophy, literature, and psychology.[2]

The philosophical critiques targeted belief that there are universal and innate feelings of sympathy (*tongqingxin*). The Maoists called that thesis "the humanism that emerges from human nature." The Maoists considered the behavioral implication of this doctrine to be that the people will out of kindness tolerate their oppressors rather than fighting against them. It undercuts class struggle. The Maoist counter thesis is, "We do not apply a policy of benevolence to the reactionaries."[3] Even the benign claim that the preservation of life is a common instinct was attacked. The popular Peking University philosopher Feng Ding asserted that "being well fed and clothed, living in a spacious and clean house, enjoying love ..." are shared biological strivings.[4] But this goal ignores transforming people's minds for new tasks, according to the Maoists.

A traditional common claim about good literature is that, using one particular case, it can speak to the general human condition. So Ba Ren (Wang Renshu, former member of the editorial board of *Wenyi bao* [Literature and art daily] and a diplomat) said that "People all like the fragrance of flowers, the song of a bird."[5] But Maoists rejected this, as ignoring the fact that people of different classes respond to such stimuli differently. And these kind of stimuli are trivial, not essential in considering social behaviors. So a literature that concentrates on them is trivial.

In psychology, starting in 1953, visiting Soviet psychologists taught Chinese the Pavlovian idea, orthodox in the U.S.S.R., that there is a certain fixed, physical basis to human behavior in the design of the human nervous system. At the same time, the Soviet teachers stressed that the plasticity of the nervous system is more important than its fixed character. There are great possibilities for people to acquire conditioned reflexes and for these to be transformed into unconditioned reflexes. By 1958, when relations between the two countries began to experience strain, the Chinese psychologists found that even minor references to the Pavlovian thesis would elicit charges of "biologizing man," attributing universal physiological traits to humans. The biological suggested the fixed and unchangeable. Psychologists were encouraged to focus on the malleable social nature or thoughts of humans, not on their biology or physiology. The essential differences between people were said to lie not in neurologically based character types, but in their subjective class standpoint or thought. So all three fields fell into line to stress only malleability, not the fixed biological nature.[6]

Meanwhile in the West, there was a long history of philosophers and then psychologists who conveyed to the public the idea of the malleability of man using some variation on what Steven Pinker has called "the blank slate" theory.[7] Locke, Hume, and Mill were empiricists who said that we are what experience writes on our blank minds. The behaviorists John B. Watson and then B. F. Skinner reformulated the same basic principle, ignoring what might be innately imprinted in the mind. The movement reached its height with the anthropologists Boas and Durkheim claiming that our individual natures are nothing more than what social factors mold into us.[8] Human commonalities, or a common human nature, would deal only with trivial matters. The differences between cultures are what counts, and those differences have no biological basis.

This perspective was the inheritance of some of the most prominent actors in the subsequent Western fight against reintroducing biological universals into the topic of human nature. However, beginning in the 1970s, there was a new ingredient in the arguments of these opponents of innate universals, such as Stephen Jay Gould and Richard Lewontin. Their targets were the sociobiologists, led by E. O. Wilson. What was new was political concerns of a kind that occurred in China during the Maoist years. So here is a context into which to fit that issue in Maoism. These concerns are that for some people a biological approach to human nature ignores the political interest in the changeability of people and with it the improvement of existing social conditions. The opponents charged the sociobiologists with racism, with wanting to retain the existing social and economic inequalities. Instead, the opponents say nothing is fixed. Culture, not biology, supremely affects and makes all of us different. And being Westerners, they believed in a completely free will. We are free to change ourselves and free to change the world. We can hold responsible and blame people who believe in a fixed nature for their role in obstructing change. Malleability triumphs over any fixed biological nature.[9] Culture is all, or, as in the Maoist position, the social nature of man is all.

The opponents' political agenda has not been lost on the advocates of sociobiology (or evolutionary biology or evolutionary psychology, or behavioral ecology). They are aware of Noam Chomsky's statement that the blank slate brain is a dictator's dream.[10] It elevates the rank and role of the "educators" who manipulate the minds of others for society's good.

BOTH MALLEABILITY AND THE FIXED NATURE

Most scientists now share the approach that human nature is a product of the environment (including culture) and genes, and that means often of the two interacting. This certainly is the position of sociobiologists such as E. O. Wilson. Seymour Benzer, one of the twentieth century's greatest biologists, studied the link of genes and behavior by breeding mutant fruit flies. About his work one writer says, "In a quiet way, the molecular biologists were doing work that would eventually help to vindicate Wilson and some of the aims of sociobiology."[11]

Here again we find one of the many factors that show how some of Confucian ethics is consistent with the actual human condition. The Mencian portrait combines the confidence in education that goes along with belief in malleability, with the belief that there is also an inborn or fixed basis for some social behavior, in the "four minds." The ultimate foundation of ethics lies not in a supernatural being or realm, but in what the early Confucians called the original mind found in us all at birth, and today we would call biology.

The contemporary scientific position anchors malleability in three domains. The first is the plasticity of the neural pathways in the brain. There are great variations in the pathways used by neurotransmitters, different versions of the same genetic sequence, which allow for different ways in which the pathways interact. This opens the door biologically for vast differences in personalities.[12] Genes work in teams to produce an organism that flexibly can work in different types of environment.[13] Reference here is to short term malleability that can affect individuals differently. Organisms, such as sponges, are also subject to long term, sometimes continuous, changes in the way they express the genes in their genetic code, that is in how they act and look. Temperature might be the factor causing the change. Such "phenotypic plasticity" is not of interest to those with political agendas.[14] But the malleability of the neural pathways is of interest, because it means that educators who convey to students the experience of other humans, can indeed foster the growth of new cortical neurons. Experience, direct or indirect, strengthens neurons that otherwise would atrophy.[15] So the second domain in which malleability is based is the impact of educational experience on the brain.

But remember that learning from an educator or from other experience also depends on the genes and the neural circuitry that they help create. Back and forth influences.

There is a third reason for retaining malleability in the mix of it with the biologically innate. It is the relative unpredictability of much, but certainly not all, individual human behavior. In part this is because a single nerve cell can get information from many neurons, all subject to alteration by experience.[16] Brain chemistry is constantly impacted by social events. Also, our mind is made up of competing factions.[17] Genes give us selfish motives, and yet also the ability to love and to care for justice. Choice is a fact of human life and is the most proximate, experienced source of our great distance from being only a fixed quantity. Genes often do not operate at all unless signaled to do so by our choices. Natural selection may ease us into behavior that reinforces our reproductive fitness, but we can choose patterns of behavior that go against it, as in the decision to remain childless. Studies of our child-rearing practices and legal system show that people do build into their decisions a sense of the consequences of their actions. We hold individuals responsible, providing they can be aware of the consequences of their decisions to act.[18] Feelings, located in identifiable brain regions, assist us in making choices and help our foresight. Sometimes those feelings are within our control, as we decide which emotionally laden things to allow near us.[19] Books to read and friends with whom to interact are within our control. Mencius realized this.

But contrary to the perspective of some dictators and social scientists who believe "only culture counts," there are limits to our malleability. Our genetic makeup does establish behavior tendencies or patterns or predispositions to certain forms of social behavior. E. O. Wilson would identify such examples as parental investment in offspring, altruism, avoidance of incest, cooperation, and contract making.[20] Others add to the list the quest for esteem and autonomy.[21] In other words, these fixed elements in our natures predispose us (not force us) to make certain choices. This does not deny that predispositions are subject to environmental influence. Nature and nurture are both involved. The predispositions do not determine our conduct. But they are certainly relevant to any description of what we are as humans. The predispositions make it easy for us to perform and build upon certain types of behavior. And they increase the likelihood that social policies that go against the predispositions will fail. Recall the failure of the Maoist communal kitchens and some of the kibbutz communal child rearing practices in Israel. You generally cannot fight family bonds successfully.

In the end, the findings of evolutionary biology help us to identify what the strengths and weaknesses are of some fundamentals of Mencian Confucianism. One of these is the power of the predisposition to acts of reciprocal altruism among kin. The power of social networks in Chinese society is well known. Many are modeled on the family analogy, though not necessarily involving genetic kin. Especially when legal authorities are weak, they provide protections and services. But such in-group/out-group boundaries also obstruct the flow of information that obstructs good problem solving and the growth of new knowledge. The boundaries limit the number of people and variety of perspectives brought to bear on an issue. They also foster cronyism and corruption. At the same time, the survival and multiplication and strength of the Chinese people at the group and individual level owe much to the importance of lineages in which the biological principles of kin selection operate. In practice, these often employ the psychology of relationships similar to those in the networks. As a result, there are special feelings and benefits provided to kin. As one biologist puts it,

> [S]election has evidently favored people with the motivational mechanisms, emotional systems, and intellectual capacities that enable us to learn kinship categories, establish links with others, educate others about genealogical relationships, and feel a sense of solidarity and cooperativeness with those identified as relatives, especially with our close relatives.[22]

Mencian Confucians, whether at the philosophical or popular social level would not quarrel with this statement. And much of traditional Chinese education has concerned passing on information about how to organize society with interpersonal rituals that solidify the kinship categories. It has helped the occupants of those categories survive.

Western Sinology

8

Recent Western Scholarship Relevant to Chinese Philosophy

ANALYSIS

As I have thought about modern Western works relevant to Chinese philosophy, three themes continue to emerge. At least one of them pops up in almost every book. In the following pages, I give examples of works that illustrate this matter. In this analysis I illustrate by referring to specific authors as examples. These authors and their works are identified by numbers that correspond to the full description and evaluation of the works in the pages following the analysis.

The first of these themes is the focus on one form of Confucianism, to the exclusion of other forms. From this fact I infer that Western scholars believe in the usefulness of making definitional distinctions between the various forms in order to distinguish differences among schools that have the same name. The second theme is the difference between philosophy as theory and philosophy in action. The same Chinese thinker or the same Western analyst may have one point of view when explaining a principle, but a very different one when dealing with that principle in action. The third is consistency. Some analysts ask if an original author's work or an original doctrine was or was not internally consistent This is directly related to the issue of whether ideas change over time and, if so, how significantly. We should evaluate the degree to which consistency and change over time are important in discussing positions.

---

* First published as "Sange zhuti ji daibiao zuo" (Three themes and their representative authors), in *Zhongguo zhexueshi* (History of Chinese philosophy), 1 (2003), pp. 20–28.

I begin with the different forms of Confucianism. In my own analysis, there are significant differences between state or imperial Confucianism, popular or family centered Confucianism, and the philosophical kind. State Confucianism was first implemented by the Emperor Wu in the Former Han and received its ideological foundation from Dong Zhongshu. In values, it emphasizes loyalty to the emperor as the main virtue for individuals. For society as a whole, it stresses uniformity of mind (*da yitong*) as a means of ensuring order or harmony in the realm. Its method of attaining that uniformity is through establishing schools, then controlling the curriculum in schools, through civil service examinations for positions of privilege based on a knowledge of that official curriculum, and through state controlled market town lectures for illiterates. The works of Peter Bol on Wang Anshi illustrate both this form, and the opposition to it by people such as Sima Guang (no. 4). Similarly, when John Dardess (no. 7) discusses the autocratic nature of Ming Taizu's ideas about education, he is dealing with another exemplar of imperial Confucianism. For Taizu, education is not helping the individual discover his own mind, but rather it is force feeding the ruler's doctrines into the minds of the people.

Popular Confucianism centers around the individual virtue of filiality and the family virtue of familial harmony. These are attained through the fulfillment of traditional family social roles. It is also concerned with the preservation of family property. Robert Hymes (no. 3) is dealing with this form in his work on the scholar-officials of an area in Jiangxi in the Southern Song.

Philosophical Confucianism eventually came to draw heavily on the tradition of Mencius. It bases its ethics on theories of human nature. In the Song-Ming periods, it is also concerned with the relation between humans and a non-empirical, transcendental Heaven. That relationship is often described as simultaneously also involving some degree of immanence of Heaven in humans. The individual virtues include reciprocal altruism (*ren*) and sincerity (*cheng*), attainable either through study of texts, moral intuition, or good works, or some combination of them. The society virtues are propriety (*li*) in behavior by all people, as a function of their social relationships, and order in the world as a whole, based on the analogy between order in family and in society at large (emphasis on hierarchy and patriarchy). The Brooks's book on the *Analects* (no. 1) deals with some kinds of philosophical Confucianism in the pre-Qin period. Thomas Metzger's *Escape from Predicament* (no. 5) is concerned with philosophical Confucianism as represented by Zhu Xi and Wang Yangming.

The second theme is the relation between philosophical positions as theory and as implemented in reality. For example, in the United States, a number of our founders, and also honored statesmen such as Abraham Lincoln, accepted the idea that "all men are created equal." They derived this from John Locke and from the religious and philosophical argument that God loves all souls equally, having created them in His image. However, they did not always treat black Americans or women in accordance with that principle. In the case of Confucians, it is certainly true that many of them promoted universal reciprocal altruism, toward people and all creatures. This is the case with Zhu Xi, Zhang Zai, Lu Jiuyuan, and Wang Yangming. The forty-seventh *zhuan* of *Zhuzi chuanshu* (Collected works of Master Zhu) is devoted to *ren* (humaneness), to be applied as affection for kin, then for the people, and finally as humane treatment of other living things. This is the message taught to and generally accepted by most scholar-officials from the Song onwards. However, the studies of Robert P. Hymes (no. 3) reveal that in actuality the concerns of Song officials were often limited to humane acts toward people in the counties for which they had responsibilities or in which their families lived. The implication was that the sage did not have to be concerned with the world at large but could focus on being a sage at home. Even the brother of Lu Jiuyuan placed primary emphasis on preserving family property, and gave merely utilitarian arguments to justify acts of charity. The de Bary study of late Ming thought (no. 6) explores how the sagely ideal of Wang Yangming changed due to practical experiences among some later scholars influenced by Wang. For example, Wang Gen said that any local commoner could become a sage. This reflected his own practical experience as a teacher of Buddhists, Daoists, laymen, monks, and Confucian scholars. It is quite different from Wang Yangming's own position that, though people of modest intelligence and the sage all share innate knowledge, only the sage can act on that knowledge. Wang's implication is that there are not many of those sages.

The third and final theme in these works involves examining whether or not the ideas of a given text or thinker or school are internally consistent. Authors have different purposes for such projects. One is to support a thesis about how ideas evolved over time. In the case of the Brooks's work on the *Analects* (no. 1), inconsistencies in chapters are evidence of the presence of insertions from later time periods. Liu Xiaogan (no. 2) offers counter arguments that the same bamboo texts from the Warring States period contain inconsistent passages. Benjamin Elman (no. 8) focuses on the changes over time in New Text thought. The later New Text thinkers advocate horizontal alliances of like-minded people to preserve the intellectual legacy, not the clan based guardianship of an earlier period. And the later New Text thinkers advocate statecraft activities not found in the philologically oriented works of earlier members of the school. Guy Alitto (no. 10) studied the ideas of "intuition" and of cultural blending of essentials from Western and Chinese cultures, in the thought of Liang Shuming. He found that Liang's positions in the 1930s had varied considerably from his earlier ones. A similar purpose in studying internal consistency is to determine how close in time and in philosophical agreement one set of passages is to another. For example, when Liu Xiaogan found about ninety passages in Chapters 22–27 of the Outer and Miscellaneous Chapters of the *Zhuangzi* that are identical or correspond to those in the Inner Chapters, he concluded that they were written by disciples of Zhuangzi who lived near in time to the master and shared his ideas. A. C. Graham (no. 2) takes a similar position.

The other purpose in looking at the question of consistency is to use it as a basis for critical evaluation. This is the case with Benjamin Schwartz in his book on Yan Fu (no. 9). For Schwartz, when Yan Fu tries to harmonize borrowings from Mill and Spencer he is trying to harmonize inconsistent and incompatible positions. I would conclude by saying that I find no problem with the first purpose for being concerned with consistency, but I do with the second. The second applies a Western standard of evaluating theories and ignores the standard that has long been in use in China. That Chinese standard is: What theory can best motivate people to act (in the case of Yan Fu, act to save China)?

In summary, my analysis reveals three topics that run through many of the Western works on Chinese philosophy: definitions and their utility in making distinctions between schools with the same name, the differences between the same philosophical positions as theory and as practice, and internal consistency within an original text. We can go beyond Chinese philosophy and say that these are topics for analysis for studying Western philosophy as well, because they raise similar questions in both areas about each culture's traditional classics. These three topics do not know cultural boundaries.

EXAMPLES CITED BY NUMBER IN THE ANALYSIS

1. E. Bruce Brooks and A. Takeo Brooks, *The Original Analects: Sayings of Confucius and His Successors* (New York: Columbia University Press, 1998)

This is a translation and commentary on the *Analects*. It is also a new theory about how the text was put together and about whose ideas are in it. Its thesis opposes the traditional position that "the text was put together over a relatively short time, and could thus still plausibly be regarded as reflecting, in its entirety, the thought and career of the historical Confucius" (p. 339). Instead, on the basis of inconsistencies in the text, it argues that the traditional text is composed of layers, and alterations or insertions in those layers. The insertions belonged originally in other layers from the ones in which they now exist. The Brookses acknowledge that their theory owes a debt to the Qing scholar Cui Shu (1740–1816) and to Gu Jiegang (1893–1980), leader of the "doubting antiquity" movement of the 1920s and 1930s.

This approach is significant for philosophy because it tries to show how Confucian doctrine evolved over time. This applies to the meaning and centrality (or absence of centrality) of certain terms. The authors illustrate this point with the case of *ren*. They say that (1) originally it was associated with the warrior code of honor (so it meant being steadfast or successful in the face of adversity) (pp. 14–15). (2) Then, in the Fourth Century B.C., a new value system arose, centering on *li* (ritual rules). *Ren* was ignored (*Analects* 10, 11). (3) Finally, under Mohist influence, the school of Mencius returned to *ren*, but this time with the sense of benevolence or compassion (p. 254) (*Analects* 12.22 and 13, dating from 326–322 B.C.).

The insertions were made by members of the Lu school over a period of 230 years, from the death of Confucius in 479 until the extinction of the Lu school in 249 B.C.

Evaluation: There is much in the Brooks's book with which I agree. For example, we agree that Confucians both emphasized inborn instincts to do good and also say people's natures are malleable, a function of education and of environmental deprivation. We also agree that they stressed education as a workable form of political control. At the same time, I call attention to Liu Xiaogan, who has criticized the Brooks's position on the basis of three points. (1) The Brookses rely too much on the authority of the "doubting antiquity" movement, which focused only on texts. Liu accepts the alternative view of Wang Guowei (1877–1927) that one should use the double evidence of bones/bronzes/archaeological finds, and of texts. (2) The Brookses believe that the more textual material there is, the later is the time from which it comes. Regarding the *Analects*, this means that it expanded in length over time. They say it had a constant growth of two chapters in twenty-eight years, with the gradual "accretion" of chapters. But Liu replies, there were many texts even in the period near the time of Confucius. The bamboo slips from Guodian reveal that the existing texts about which we know are only a tiny fraction of the actual legacy. The slips reveal many texts not even included in the Han bibliographies. We can trust those bibliographies that the *Analects* as a whole is early. (3) The Brookses regard inconsistencies in a text as evidence of later insertions. But the bamboo slips reveal that one text often contains apparent inconsistencies as a part of the basic work.

2. Angus Graham, *Chuang-tzu: The "Inner Chapter"* (London: George Allen and Unwin, 1981); and "How Much of *Chuang-tzu* Did Chuang-tzu Write," in Henry Rosemont and Benjamin Schwarz eds., *Studies in Classical Chinese Thought: Papers Presented at the Workshop on Classical Chinese Thought Held at Harvard University, August 1976* (Chicago: American Academy of Religion, 1979)

One of Graham's major theses concerns the classification and dating of the Outer and Miscellaneous Chapters of the *Zhuangzi*. He identifies four classes of passages: (1) Passages that have a direct connection to those in the Inner Chapters. (2) Chapters that idealize a tribal utopia with no social distinctions, where men live as spontaneously as animals. They also contain the theme that when rulers apply punishments and when people try to use reasoning, spontaneity is disrupted. Graham calls these the "Primitivist" passages (including all of chapters 8–10 and part of 11) and dates them to 209–202 B.C. (3) Chapters that prize an individual caring for his body and avoiding risk, so as to live out his allotted term. They show a preference for private life rather than a life in public service. These are non-Daoist. Graham calls them "Yangist." They include chapters 28–31 and date from after 200 B.C. (4) "Syncretist" chapters, that combine a respect for Legalist administrative techniques, Confucian benevolence (*ren*) and ritual rules (*li*), and the following of *wuwei* by the ruler. They idealize the Yellow Emperor and Yao and Shun.

Evaluation: Liu Xiaogan's own classification of the *Zhuangzi* chapters agrees in its broad outlines with Graham. But Liu has the following specific critiques of Graham, with which I agree: (1) None of the Outer or Miscellaneous chapters date from later than 235 B.C., which is when the compiler of the *Lüshi chunqiu*, Lü Buwei, died. His text dates from 240 B.C. Liu's evidence is, first, a statistical count of the *Zhuangzi* passages quoted in *Lüshi chunqiu*, and, second, the presence in the Outer and Miscellaneous chapters of compounds (such as *daode*) that appeared as single characters (*de*) in the Inner Chapters. (2) As for Graham's "Syncretist" classification, Liu says there was no such term in use in the classical period. But there was a term "Huang-Lao" and a description of what Huang-Lao people believed, by Sima Tan. So it is better to use that term. Liu says that their ideas can be found in chapters 12–16, 33 and the end of 11. (3) As for Graham's "Yangist" class, Liu says that there is no consistent prizing of either life or of the self in these chapters. There is no justification for introducing another new term, "Yangist," that did not exist at the time in question. Liu and Graham agree that chapters 17–22 (Liu adds chapters 23–27 and 32) belong to the transmitters of Zhuangzi's ideas who lived closest in time to him and whose ideas most closely resemble those of the Inner Chapters. Liu bases this in part of finding about ninety passages in chapters 17–27 that are identical or correspond to those in the Inner Chapters.

3.   Robert P. Hymes, *Statesmen and Gentlemen: The Elite of Fu-chou, Chiang-hsi, in Northern and Southern Sung* (Cambridge: Cambridge University Press, 1986)

The focus of this book is on the implications for Confucianism of a new focus on local communities by scholar-officials of the Southern Song. It is particularly useful for understanding the content of the idea of the sage and his virtue of *ren* (humaneness) in Song Neo-Confucianism. The ideal goal of the sage was to benefit by humane acts the family, the people, and all creatures. But in actuality the concerns of Confucian officials was limited to humane acts toward people in the counties (*xiang*) for which they had responsibilities or in which their families lived. The implication is that the idea of the sage's interests became localized, and the message is that it is possible to be a sage at home, rather than only in the world at large.

Regarding Zhu Xi, Hymes describes his support for the community contract (*xiangyue*) and for communal granaries (which charged no interest to local farmers at planting time). These benefit primarily the residents of a *xiang*. Hymes argues that Zhu Xi was trying to fill a gap left by a weakened central authority, the imperial court. Regarding other elites, Hymes shows that they did not in fact give high priority to the value of *ren* or universal altruism. Their dominant values were those of fulfilling family social roles and preserving family property. Using as an example the brother of Lu Jiuyuan, Hymes shows that the main argument for justifying acts of charity was utilitarian, not following the model of sages. That utilitarian argument was that one should give to the needy rather than risk conflict with those people and others who expect you to do charitable giving.

Hymes identifies three historical factors that transformed the sagehood ideal away from being attainable only through imperial court service or some other vehicle that would give one access to "all under heaven." (1) One was the weak power of central government authorities in applying policy in local areas. This reduced the need for local gentry to seek close personal relationships with central authorities. (2) Next, there were factional struggles that made high office at court seem to local officials to be a dangerous course for their sons to choose. (3) Finally, the social disorders of the Southern Song generated some fears about holding on to family wealth, thereby encouraging people to seek the preservation of property as a primary goal.

The result was that individuals sought sagehood at home rather than as part of the bureaucracy. Hymes highlights the fact that their models were exemplary local officials, "True Confucians" (*zhenru*), who love the local people as parents do their own children.

Evaluation: This book provides concrete evidence of certain cases in which there is a difference between the Confucian orthodoxy to which gentry gave nominal assent, and their actual application of the principles in those teachings. It is always useful for the philosopher to remember that philosophical terms and ideals change under different historical circumstances. The language may be constant and consistent with earlier classics, but not the meaning. This book gives examples in the case of the ideal of the sage, whose concerns in this case shift from all under Heaven to local people.

4. Peter Bol, "Government, Society, and State: The Political Visions of Ssu-ma Kuang and Wang An-shih," in Robert Hymes and Conrad

Shirokauer eds., *Ordering the World: Approaches to State and Society in Sung Dynasty China* (Berkeley: University of California Press, 1993); Peter Bol, *"This Culture of Ours": Intellectual Transitions in T'ang and Sung China* (Stanford: Stanford University Press, 1992)

A central theme in Bol's work is the imperial Confucian principle that politics and morality should be unified, so that high and low share the same values. This principle assumes that there is no other way to attain the ideal of "unifying the world." Bol deals with the topic by analyzing descriptions of policies implemented by Wang to achieve the unification, by uncovering the aims of those policies, and by presenting Sima Guang's critique of those policies.

(1) Description: Antiquity (i.e. West Zhou) provides the model for organizing the society and state into one system. The sages of antiquity are the models for how to carry it out. We learn from them that "divergent opinions" should be stamped out. On this foundation in 1068, Wang ordered action in education, the civil service, agriculture, military, and financial matters.

(2) Aims: The first aim is to transform the characters of the "gentlemen scholars" (*shi*) who are the traditional moral elite, so that, as in ancient times, they can serve as exemplars for the society. This transformation is to be achieved in government schools, after which they will work in the civil service. Independent minded officials who do not share the uniform values taught in those schools should be suppressed. The second aim is to minimize or eliminate divisions between the people so as to make an integrated social order receptive to commands from above. This can be achieved by turning farmers at the same time also into soldiers and police. It is also necessary to suppress people of independent wealth on whom the poor are dependent; their existence creates a source of power in competition with the imperial court. This is called "managing wealth." The two aims will be attained when there is no opposition to the government, a situation called "unity of morality and a change of customs."

(3) Critique by Sima Guang: Presented in memorials of 1069 and 1085. Eliminating the division of labor eliminates the specialized knowledge necessary to perform tasks and causes central

officials to interfere with local problems about which they know little. So the central Finance Commission should not interfere with local officials or with the people's economic activities. Farmers should stick to farming and soldiers/police to jobs for which they were trained. As for eliminating the rich-poor division, managing wealth was not a concern of the ancient sages, so there is no need for contemporaries to attend to it.

Evaluation: Bol's work reminds us that we should make distinctions between the different kinds of Confucianism that existed over the course of Chinese history. These include philosophical, popular, and state Confucianism. Wang Anshi is an example of state Confucianism, which often prized uniformity of beliefs and loyalty as the primary values. These differ fundamentally from the priorities of popular Confucianism (family cohesiveness, filiality, preservation of family property, and perpetuating the family line as established by ancestors), and philosophical Confucianism (the unity of heaven and humans and an ethics based on human nature, with special attention to self-cultivation as a means to sagehood).

5.   Thomas A. Metzger, *Escape from Predicament: Neo-Confucianism and China's Evolving Political Culture* (New York: Columbia University Press, 1977)

Metzger says that his analysis derives from a predicament noted by Tang Junyi, that is found in Confucianism from the Southern Song onwards. Metzger applies the analysis to Zhu Xi and also refers to Wang Yangming. The predicament that supposedly is found in the works of Zhu Xi and his followers is this. The same Heaven that facilitates the attainment of the supreme goal of world harmony can also obstruct it. This means that in working for the goal, people can draw on the moral power of Heaven, a transcendent cosmic force. But that same Heaven can hinder individuals from obtaining the moral power. In terms of China's specific history, Zhu Xi and his followers were so disappointed with the failure of Wang Anshi's attempted reforms that they did not seek the road to world harmony in the outer realm of political and economic affairs. Instead, they turned to the inner life of moral striving for mental clarity and intuitive knowledge. At the same time, however, they believed that material desires obstruct people from understanding the cosmic good.

Also, Heaven can put unpredictable barriers in front of people who seek the good. So Metzger regards Zhu Xi and followers as very pessimistic about the human ability to realize Confucian ideals.

Beginning in the late nineteenth century, some Chinese found an escape from this predicament. Thanks to Western technology and forms of political participation, some Chinese intellectuals were able to ignore the failures of Wang Anshi. They had new technical and political means of dealing with the outer realm. Thus, for them, the inner problem of moral purification and of relating to a transcendent Heaven became less central. Kang Youwei is an example of someone advocating this renewed focus on concrete externals. For him, the transforming power of the sage is relocated in the outer physical life of the nation, not in efficacious moral effort (*gongfu*).

Evaluation: The predicament that Metzger identifies is indeed present in the Neo-Confucian writers. However, I do not believe it has the magnitude that Metzger assigns it. In short, I do not find Zhu Xi to be a pessimist. I think that the reason for this overemphasis on the obstacles to attaining Confucian goals is because Metzger erroneously treats the metaphysics of Zhu Xi and Wang Yangming as their core concerns. In contrast, I regard their core concerns as clarifying the mind through study (Zhu Xi) or social practice (Wang), so as to ensure the unity of knowledge and action. The evidence for Zhu's positive outlook lies in his educational (founding academies), economic (granaries), and political (community compact) efforts discussed in the Hymes book. Also in his lifelong work as a teacher.

6. "Individualism and Humanitarianism in Late Ming Thought," in W. T. de Bary ed., *Self and Society in Ming Thought* (New York: Columbia University Press, 1970)

De Bary gives the reader an example of one kind of Chinese individualism. Initially inspired by Wang Yangming, it evolved in the sequential lives and works of three persons: Wang Gen (1483?–1540), He Xinyin (1517–1579), and Li Zhi (1527–1602). There are not many counterparts in China to the individualism advocated by the German Romantics, but in the Taizhou (named after Wang Gen's hometown) school it exists. From among the set of values we normally associate with individualism, it especially prizes uniqueness, a passionate engagement in life, and self-chosen values to guide that life. The economic prosperity of the lower Yangzi (Yangtze) valley had allowed increasing numbers of people to participate in cultural activity, including commoners and those critical of asceticism that suppresses the emotions.

(1) Wang Gen. When he lived, many associated sagehood with membership in the scholar-official class. In contrast, Wang saw the road to the social ideal of order as depending on turning commoners into sages.

Each person in the lowest economic class should cultivate himself, and in return, the rulers should assume the duty of guaranteeing the welfare of such individuals. In his own life, Wang successfully taught people of a variety of social groups, including laymen and monks, Buddhists and Daoists, scholars and officials. His message was that the ultimate authority lies in each individual's mind.

(2) He Xinyin. Believing that serving as an educator contributes more to good government than does serving as an official in the bureaucracy, He advocated rejecting official posts. He himself had won first place in the Jiangxi provincial examinations and abandoned plans for an official career. Instead he made an independent career of public lecturing and teaching in private academies, where some freedom of teaching and discussion was possible.

(3) Li Zhi. Trained in the Confucian classics, he passed the provincial examination in 1552 and spent thirty years as a low level official. Increasingly, he felt it impossible both to retain his individual integrity and at the same time to succeed in rising up the normal official ladder in the usual way. Posted to Yunnan, he discovered an identity with the uneducated people around him. Eventually he repudiated the Confucian morality and Neo-Confucianism in which he had been trained. Its content was replaced by "consciousness," in the Chinese Buddhist sense in which it is devoid of customary moral categories. Opposing the authority of the Confucian classics, he endorsed a life full of emotional engagement and the expression of uniqueness by each individual as he fulfills his own goals and seeks his own values. These cannot be taught. Li Zhi rejects the Wang Yangming assumption that all people who think clearly will come to intuit the same values. There are no eternal models. They differ in each historical period. One should not follow the example of scholar-officials, most of whom are hypocrites, or even look for sages among the common people, but look to the spirit of heroes willing to break with tradition, as found in the *Shuihuzhuan*.

Evaluation: De Bary's own critiques of the weaknesses of each of these three teachings is sound. For example, in the case of He Xinyin, he writes that historically it was difficult for the academies that he prized to remain independent of rulers. There was no middle class to support their independence. In Li Zhi's case, he advocates a form of individualism that takes no account of the need for law and stable institutions. There are individualistic values that are compatible with laws, which may even protect those values. Therefore, Li Zhi's version will not be practical. I add that de Bary's work helps to distinguish different core ideas in different examples of individualism and to identify a historical period when some of those core ideas flourished. So we are better able to talk about the meaning and existence of individualism in China. In short, individualism is not only a Western value. Its *emphasis* is a modern Western phenomenon.

7. John W. Dardess, *Confucianism and Autocracy: Professional Elites in the Founding of the Ming Dynasty* (Berkeley: University of California Press, 1983)

This book is based on research into the Zhedong circuit of Zhejiang, where Ming Taizu cooperated with Confucian elites, who influenced his style of rule. It focuses on the kind of Confucianism that I have described as "imperial Confucianism," which first emerged in Han China. The main thesis is that the autocratic centralization of the early Ming is not simply an idea of the founder of the Ming. It owes its theoretical basis to doctrines of the Zhedong writers, such as Liu Ji (1311–1375), who assigned great power to the emperor. Two of their ideas stand out. One is that Chinese masses are stupid. They require that "… the ruler/teacher completes the people. If they do not respond, though they are called 'men,' they are indistinguishable from beasts." The other is that China's educated elites (referring to the *shi* or *ru*) who become officials, are usually corrupt. Bureaucratic corruption caused the collapse of the Yuan dynasty.

Starting from this perspective, Ming Taizu took as his goals transforming the masses of people in accord with ancient moral values, and causing the officials to be of one mind with the ruler. The primary means to attain the goal would be for himself (and future rulers) to serve as a teacher whose core policies would be educational. Thereby the cloudy or selfish minds of the people would be eliminated and their original goodness restored. To this end, he ordered schools established in all prefectures and counties to prepare students to compete to enter the imperial university. And in 1391 schools were established in all tax districts.

The author then shows that Ming Taizu's idea of education was very autocratic, the opposite of training people to seek truth in themselves. The key to education for everyone was Taizu's own treatise, the "Great Announcement" (*dagao*). The curriculum in the schools set up in 1391 focused on the Great Announcement. Every three years, teachers would bring pupils to the capital for contests in reciting the Announcement. In 1397, 193,400 teachers and students came to the capital for the contest. Ming Taizu also employed other traditional social control and indoctrination techniques that rely on community pressure: the village ceremonial wine drinking (*xiangyinjiuli*) and public dishonor rolls (*shenmingting*). There was no place for an independent bureaucracy that could also serve as teachers. Most officials and the people are puppets, whose ropes and strings are pulled by the emperor. Success is due to the self control and discipline of the very few, not to the receptivity of the majority to moral suasion.

Evaluation: This book shows the continued evolution of the content of "imperial Confucianism," going beyond the Han focus on loyalty as the primary value and on the Three Bonds as the basic social relationships. It explains how the Confucian idea of teaching, as the major duty of an activist sage, undergoes a transformation in its content. There is no interest in helping the individual discover his own mind. Rather, teaching is force feeding the ruler's doctrines into the minds of the people. Mindful of this, we also learn why so many Confucians then stopped opposing imperial despotism. They were afraid of the punishments for deviating from imperial orthodoxy.

8.   Benjamin A. Elman, *From Philosophy to Philology: Intellectual and Social Aspects of Change in Late Imperial China* (Cambridge, MA: Harvard University Press, 1984); and *Classicism, Politics, and Kinship: The Ch'ang-Chou School of New Text Confucianism in Late Imperial China* (Berkeley: University of California Press, 1990)

The central themes of these works is the reemergence and subsequent development of the New Text School in late imperial China. Thereby, it provides new background material for understanding the meaning of "New Text School" and also the teachings of Kang Youwei.

The first stage in the reemergence is the appearance in the sixteenth century of the school of philology or Han Learning. This school opposed the Zhu Xi school of Neo-Confucianism. The author explains their method of using philology as a tool for debating matters of political legitimacy and government controlled interpretation of texts. Specifically, he refers to the importance of the discovery by Meizu (fl. 1513) that a famous passage used by those Neo-Confucians from a supposed early classic is in fact a forgery. This is the passage, "The human mind is dangerous; the *dao*-mind is subtle. Concentrate [the *dao*-mind], be single-minded. Sincerely grasp the mean" (from the "Da Yu mo" section of the *Book of History*). As interpreted by some of the Neo-Confucians, the passage elevates introspection, denigrates human desires in favor of frugality, and advocates the authoritarianism of a one-minded society. By using philology as a tool to show that the passage is a forgery, the philologists were able to attack those Neo-Confucian values.

The second stage is the acquisition of statecraft (*jingshi*, "to order the world") concerns in addition to those concerning philology. Examples of the statecraft concerns include flood control and map making. These special interests were adopted by specific lineages or clans.

Stage three in the author's analysis is the adoption of two models in the nineteenth century. Curiously, although the philologists opposed Zhu Xi, people associated with the first of the two models selected in the nineteenth century praised him. This first model is the early seventeenth century Donglin School, members of which wished to restore social stability by restoring Song Confucian *daoxue* orthodoxy and had no interest in institutional reform. For the New Text scholars, the Donglin people were a model of a horizontal alliance (a faction) of men of virtuous character who shared one-mind or the same values. Thus, although in the late Ming and early Qing, the New Text School was located in specific lineages or clans, it gradually evolved into non-clan based, horizontal alliances of like minded persons. The immediate stimulus was opposition to a corrupt imperial retainer in the late eighteenth century, seemingly analogous to the Donglin opposition to a corrupt eunuch official in their time. The other model in this third stage was the new group of statecraft reformers, who advocated institutional reform. They focused on matters such as land registration and tax controls. So from the Donglin school comes the model of the horizontal alliance not based on clans. But in addition, the New Text scholars adopted from the other model something the Donglin people did not share, namely the statecraft concerns.

Evaluation: These works provide the richest account in a Western language of the content and evolution of the New Text School teachings.

Elman explains the different functions of philology and statecraft in the pursuit of practical goals concerning the improvement of Chinese society. They also reveal how the doctrines of Zhu Xi were very much alive at this time, although used for different purposes at different times.

9.   Benjamin Schwartz, *In Search of Wealth and Power: Yen Fu and the West* (Cambridge, MA: Harvard University Press, 1964)

This work begins with a description of Yan Fu's goal and of the means he proposes for achieving it. The goal is the survival of a nation-state, specifically China, by enhancing its wealth and power. The means is to understand and embody the essential values of Western political culture: freedom, self interest, and struggle. Then Chinese should combine them with one Confucian value: *shu* (sympathetic reciprocity). All of these values are means to state wealth and power.

The book's other theme is a critical evaluation of Yan Fu's theories. The criticism is based on what Schwartz considers to be two errors of Yan Fu. (1) Yan Fu misunderstands some of the key Western value terms, as used by the Western philosophers he cites. For example, J. S. Mill's "freedom" refers to minimal societal rules obstructing what an individual believes and a relative absence of barriers to the individual's life style. For Mill the result is that the right ideas and the best life styles win out in competition with other ones and thereby promote progress. The benefit goes to the individual and to society, not to the nation-state. However, Yan Fu interprets Mill as advocating the elimination of obstructions to people using their abilities, so that their energy will be released to help the nation in its struggles. From Spencer, Yan Fu borrows self-interest and struggle. But, contrary to Spencer, who does not concern himself with the nation-state, Yan Fu treated self-interest and struggle as being in the service of the survival and supremacy of the Chinese state as it competes with other states. (2) The other error that Schwartz attributes to Yan Fu is internal inconsistency. For example, he says that Yan Fu tries to harmonize Mill and Spencer. But their basic principles are in fact incompatible: Spencer favors but Mill opposes self-interest. Mill favors as the ultimate standard the greatest happiness of the greatest number. Another example is that Yan Fu is an organicist in his metaphysics, and that is compatible with the value of *shu*. But it is not compatible with the value of self-interest, to which Yan Fu is also attached. Self-interest may destroy the harmony of society's parts.

Evaluation: On the positive side, Schwartz shows the complexity in Yan Fu's thought. We should not assign simple labels to him. Is he "conservative"? Yes, but only that part that believes in progress through slow steps on the analogy of biological evolution. Is he a "radical"? Yes, but only that part that is concerned with the struggle and competition in which China must engage in order to survive among other nations. On the negative side, to criticize Yan Fu for lack of consistency is to apply a basic Western standard for evaluating theories and to ignore the standard that has long been in use in China: What theory can best motivate people to act, in the case of Yan Fu "to act to save China"?

I would offer another critique of Yan Fu, rather than of Schwartz. He did not take the trouble to outline a program of political change, as Liang Qichao did (such as implementing an independent judiciary, a parliament, and representative government), along with guidance as to how to achieve it. For example, people need to think about who decides when there is a conflict of individual liberty and state interest. Institutions are needed, such as watchdog agencies with the power to investigate government actions.

10. Guy S. Alitto, *The Last Confucian: Liang Shu-ming and the Chinese Dilemma of Modernity* (Berkeley: University of California Press, 1986)

This book shows Liang Shuming using a category that today is the subject of debate. That category is "essential," contrasted with "non-essential." Specifically, the author reveals that Liang identified certain values, mental processes, and political institutions as respectively essential to Chinese and Western culture, though their actual implementation may have been at times weak. In the case of China these include: the values of harmony and compromise; the thought process of intuition (*zhijue*) that involves emotions such as sympathy, associated with *ren* (humaneness); and the political institution of community contract (*xiangyue*), in which participation is not based on self-interest but rather on the relationship of leaders to led. In Western culture, in contrast, the core value is self-interest; the mental process is intellectual calculation of the costs and benefits of the consequences of actions (consequentialism, *gongli zhuyi*) by analysis of an object or situation into parts, leading to guidance "how to do it"; the political institutions are democratic, based on laws and the individual rights that those laws protect, rather than being based on relationships. Long lasting cultural differences exist in the West and in China as a result: Western utilitarianism justifies happiness coming from the acquisition of material objects, whereas in Confucianism, joy comes from actions themselves, not from what a person gains (the consequences or costs/benefits) by them (*wu suo wei er wei*).

The book stresses how an individual's ideas change over time. In discussing this matter, Liang assumes that there are "cultural thought processes." Chinese could make moral judgments without cost/benefit considerations. Westerners could not. For example, he focuses on the idea of intuition. Prior to 1927, Liang uses terms such as *ren* and *zhijue* to refer to moral judgments without selfish motives. After 1927, he uses *lixing. Lixing* is close to the Confucian term "public minded" (*gongxin*) and cannot be associated with individual desires, a weakness of the term *zhijue*. Prior to the 1930s, Liang is opposed to blending elements from different cultures (i.e. to blending the essentials of different cultures). After the early 1930s, he approved of it. For example, he approved of changing the content of *lixing* so that it also includes the idea of beneficial results (*gongli*). Those results are the good consequences that occur when people take account of family and social ties.

Evaluation: There may be long lasting cultural differences between China and some Western societies, as Liang suggests. This is Liang's own positive contribution. But there is no evidence for long lasting character types, which he also proposes. Even with respect to cultures, his essentialist view of thought processes ignores the empirical study of cultures, and he attributes too much causal power to styles of "thought process." In the case of China, her problems are not just in thought process but also in the causes of poverty and disease that have no necessary relation to thought processes. The social sciences, especially economics, and medicine, especially epidemiology, discover these causes of poverty and disease. An empirical study of Western cultures would have revealed non-utilitarian values that co-exist with the utilitarian ones, namely charity and public service demanded by Protestant sects, and toleration of different world views. Another positive contribution of the book itself is to show the need to be aware of how an individual's ideas and terminology evolve and change over time.

9

Yes, There Is a Core Confucianism
Out There

Not since Wm. Theodore de Bary published *The Message of the Mind in Neo-Confucianism*[1] in 1989 have I been so stimulated by a work on Chinese philosophy. That is the way I felt upon finishing a new book by Lionel Jensen. It is entitled, *Manufacturing Confucianism* (Durham: Duke University Press, 1998). The author makes his case powerfully. Yet I left the study concerned that he did his job of showing how some people have manufactured Confucianism so well that he produced a consequence that he may not have intended to produce. He left defenseless anyone who believes there is a core Confucianism distinct from the interpretations, conceptual constructions, or ideologies of the interpreters or manufacturers.

The organizing principle of Jensen's book is that Westerners and Chinese, respectively, invented Confucius (Kongzi) and Confucianism. He shows how the Jesuits turned those terms into metonyms for "Chinese," confusing a person who embodied an ethic with the ethic. In his entirely original treatment of this phenomenon, Jensen shows how the Jesuits in the field uncoupled their links with the Vatican in many respects. They viewed themselves as followers of Confucius, akin to the "order of the *ru* (ritual masters)" to which Confucius and his disciples belonged. Thus, the Jesuits and *ru*, they felt, are overlapping orders, and the *ru* could easily become Christians.

The second part of the book discusses the role of two prominent Chinese intellectuals of the first half of the twentieth century in an endeavor somewhat parallel to that of the Jesuits. One of these, Hu Shi

* First delivered as an address to the *Analects* workshop, Center for Chinese Studies, University of Michigan, March 8, 2003.

(d. 1962) found in the term *ru* something rich that he could use to fabricate a commonality of China with the West. For the Renaissance that Hu sought for China in the twentieth century, he found a precursor in the intellectual revolt of Confucius. Kongzi was a *ru* in the Shang tradition who opposed the parochialism of the dominant tribe that had conquered the Shang. Confucius becomes the symbol of an ecumenical world of humaneness, a counterpart to the Greek intellectuals who civilized their Roman conquerors. For Hu, he is also a counterpart of Jesus, who had revitalized a stodgy Judaism. Confucius brought new life to the dusty rites of the Shang, manufacturing a new tradition.

Thus, Jensen's deeper thesis is that through manufacturing Confucianism, both the European Jesuits and certain modern Chinese intellectuals undercut the foundation of the claim that China is forever qualitatively different from the West. Christianity and the ethos of the *ru* (Shininess) are part of a universal ethos, for the Jesuits and for certain modern Chinese figures. In so making his case, Jensen is arguing that there is no single essential Kongzi (Confucius), *ru*, or Shininess. These are symbols available for manufacture by people each in their own era, each in their own way. They are symbols diverse in use. Professor de Bary's focus on Neo-Confucianism as a form of individualism would be only one of the most recent examples.

This is a risky and courageous route to take. In so doing, like the finest scholars, Jensen asks some quite fundamental questions. For example: Has Confucianism become a figure of speech for "Chinese"? If so, why? His answer is yes, and the explanation centers on the accommodationist successors of Ricci. In its scope, the book covers a range of historical periods that is rare among China scholars. It is erudite, drawing on Western philosophy, the Chinese classics, and European language sources. One example can illustrate this. In order to explain the unwillingness of Jesuits to accept religious aspects of the cult of Confucius, he provides evidence from both the Italian and Latin versions of the history of the founding of the Jesuit missions in China. The book is a tour de force.

Lionel Jensen would not accept being labeled as a post-modernist. However, he makes certain assumptions, and even states them openly, that lead the reader to wonder if he is at least some kind of camp follower. In short, Jensen is marvelous when defending his thesis that Confucianism was manufactured at various times and how it was done. However, there is a problem in his claims that what we know is always mediated through prior concepts and ideology. It says that there is no Confucianism, or what the Chinese have called *ru*ism out there. This I cannot accept. Now I will explain why.

In discussing the accuracy of what and how we represent something, Jensen raises a critical issue. He says,

> This is particularly true in the case of Confucianism, because for the last three centuries it has been taken to be something "out there" in the history that the Chinese have made and continue to make. This reality does not stand alone objectively before words; it exists for us and for the Chinese insofar as it is mediated through those linguistic categories peculiar to the distinct forms of cognition we call Chinese and Western. To say this is not to deny that there is a world external to language, only that all knowledge of that world is the consequence of instinctual, mediative operations of conceptual construction.[2]

This is not true. We know some things through direct experience. When I encounter a bright light, I know it directly, not as mediated through language. The same is often true of sympathy or empathy, the reflexive experience of which is so important to Mencius.

Elsewhere, Jensen says that, "Ideology is inscribed in every discourse."[3] This also is not the case. There are physical facts about the world that are not so inscribed. These include the statements, "People die," and "The speed of light is X." It is to the presence of these physical facts about the world that I wish to turn. They are present in many societies all over the world, in most historical periods. My conclusion will be that not all of what we call Confucianism and the Chinese call *ru*ism is fabricated. Something is "out there." Specifically, it is found in the writings of the *Analects*, *Mencius*, and *Xunzi* that do more than inscribe an ideology. They point to commonalities in many societies, including those of which those *ru* had never heard. Some of these are a function of physical facts about the land and climate. Others derive from human biology. I will discuss each in turn.

Eurasia is the land mass extending from western France at one end to the east coast of China at the other. In his *Guns, Germs, and Steel: The Fates of Human Societies*,[4] Jared Diamond discusses the impact of shared geography on disparate societies, not simply China. He focuses on the accident of where certain grains and domesticatable animals appeared, and, in favorable cases, spread because the populations lived in proximate latitudes devoid of serious natural obstructions to movement. Again, if the geography was favorable, the peoples could learn from each other how to improve food production and other technologies. He finds that with excess food production, population density increases, and then a series of societal characteristics appear. The first of these is social stratification, found in chiefdoms and states. The hierarchy is ruled by what he calls a centralized kleptocracy. Excess food supports not only it but also those with job specialization skills, such as tool makers, military personnel, and priests. Religious figures help justify the centralized hierarchy. Diamond adds:

> Complex centralized societies are uniquely capable of organizing public works (including irrigation systems), long-distance trade (including the importation of metals to make better agricultural tools), and activities of different economic specialists (such as feeding herders with farmers' cereal, and transferring the herders' livestock to farmers for use as plow animals). All of these capabilities of centralized societies have fostered intensified food production and hence population growth throughout history.[5]

The second trait is ritual rules required for conflict resolution, so that people do not tear each other to shreds. These rules take account of the social roles people occupy within the hierarchy. They are usually anchored in religious practices, in that deified ancestors, especially those related to the central authority, provide their ultimate justification. Diamond says,

> ... shared ideology or religion helps solve the problem of how unrelated individuals are to live together without killing each other—by providing them with a bond not based on kinship.[6]

The two traits can be found throughout societies in Eurasia. Leaving Jared Diamond, I say that in China, the Confucians or *ru* are the ones who wrote about these, giving them interpretation and detail specific to the conditions of China and their own thinking. Those we now call Daoists opposed the hierarchies and ritual rules, opting for the simplicity, social equalities, and self sufficiency of earlier hunter-gatherer groups.

The biologically derived commonalities lead evolutionary-biologists and evolutionary psychologists to affirm that there is a human nature. They thereby invite and ward off the arrows of many scholars in the humanities and in anthropology/sociology who condemn belief in a human nature as "essentialism." The anti-essentialists focus on the differences between people and on the uniqueness of individual cultures. In reply, the Darwinian biologists and psychologists affirm the following shared traits in almost all humans: one is that what is innate and of primary moral significance is the emotions. E. O. Wilson says that "moral concepts are derived from innate emotions,"[7] thereby agreeing with Mencius for whom compassion and shame are at the center of his moral psychology. Another is that the primal emotion is infant bonding with care givers, from which compassion or sympathy is learned.

James Q. Wilson is a social scientist who draws heavily on evolutionary theory, genetics, brain science, and primatology. He joins E. O. Wilson in accepting the 1906 finding of Edward Westermarck that "the maternal sentiment is universal in mankind."[8] E. O. Wilson writes that, "Among traits with documented heritability, those closest to moral aptitude are empathy with the distress of others and certain processes of attachment between infants and their caregivers."[9]

Now to China specifically. What Mencius shares with these contemporary scientists is the affirmation that ethics can be grounded in something inborn, and it is not entirely an arbitrary human invention relative to individual communities and cultures. Ethics can be founded on something out there. Thus it is that Mencius says that the gentleman first treats his kin as kin, and then treats the people with humaneness.[10] Also, "Loving one's kin [especially parents] is humaneness."[11] E. O. Wilson puts it this way, "Kin selection [including the natural selection of genes and their effect on genetic relatives] is especially important in the origin of altruistic behavior."[12]

The *ru* always quarreled and disagreed among themselves. Xunzi remarked that there are three types of *ru*. So even at the beginning, from one perspective there is something to Lionel Jensen's warning that we should not presume a uniformity among them.[13] But this does not mean there is no common core of their beliefs. We need not accept Jensen's claim that "[Confucius] is a fetishized figure delivered from any native context in which it might embody a specific range of values or sentiments."[14] I will spell out what those commonalities are, "out there," that derive from either the consequences for food production of their shared geography or from their shared biology. They can be found in most of the pre-Qin *ru*ist texts, the *Analects*, *Mencius*, *Xunzi*, plus the fragments and essays of their disciples.

The first is that hierarchy in human society is desirable and natural. The assumption of naturalness is evident in the *Analects* passage that refers to the pole star as superior and to the fact that other stars do homage to it.[15] Other texts argue that humans should model on nature's hierarchy, represented in the status difference between heaven, which is high, and earth, which is low. Stratified social roles are called *fen* or *wei*. The common injunction is that celestial bodies, rivers, mountains, and humans should accord with the principle, "among all, each should obtain its proper position" (*jie de qi wei*).

The second commonality is the rules of behavior, the *li*, many derived from social proprieties associated with religious temple ceremonies, including weddings and funerals, treaty signing, and greeting of guests. Each of the pre-Qin *ru* texts gives prominence to the ritualized rules, which lay out forms of interaction between the occupants of the different social roles. Those concerning treaties and guests especially dramatize their function in conflict avoidance. The *ru* centered their educational activities around teaching the *li*. They were identified as teachers. In time, after China was unified, their importance as teachers was reinforced by the usefulness of their graduates as candidates for official positions.

Third, the *ru* agreed that sages of antiquity formulated and thereby justified the obligation implicit in the ritualized rules. These included the Duke of Zhou and other figures associated with the central ruling house. This includes deified royal ancestors. Once again religion is significant to support the social arrangement. Thus an acceptance of a central government as the enforcer of the rules comes with the package. Along with Confucius, who interpreted and proselytized the rules, they revered these figures as the founders of their intellectual lineage. Study of the ancients was part of their curriculum. The *ru* certainly parted company among themselves when it came to deciding which individual disciples of the founders to prize.

Fourth and finally, aware of the shared biological facts that people enter the world in the relation of infant and caregiver, and in the kinship network, the *ru* affirmed the primacy and universality of family sentiments. Kinship groups are basic to the system of social stratification. Some of the *ru* claimed that the sympathy and compassion with which individuals may treat others, including those outside of the family, derive from the kinship feelings. As the *Mencius* puts it, humaneness to others is rooted in the family. This is not to deny the coexistence of other innate social traits that the *ru* may have ignored, such as the tendency to divide into in-group and out-group sets. Further, the primacy of kinship emotions does not foreclose some loosening of their restrictions on altruism as the society grows larger. It is acceptable to be concerned about those outside the kinship group.

The conclusion is that anywhere in Eurasia where there are sedentary societies with centralized structures, whether chiefdoms or states, counterparts of these four characteristics exist, minus the nuances that are specific to China. The Confucians happen to be the people in China who focused on these four. Not everyone did. The authors of the *Daode jing* and of the Inner Chapters of the *Zhuangzi* would reject the first three of these, opting instead for the simplicity of the egalitarian social arrangements, absence of centralized authority, and minimal dominance of rules that are usually found in tribes numbering at most in the hundreds.

These, then are the facts that constitute the essentials of a *ru*ism out there. They endure in the Song and Ming. But then they become integrated as parts of a cosmic totalism. Some later Confucians taught that our minds innately carry an awareness of the objective existence of these facts, though we may momentarily be unclear about them. That is another story, involving new layers painted variously on the original facts by different new Confucians.

10

Donald Munro Answers Questions from An Yanming, for the Book, *Confucianism and Liberalism*

Q1. In the past thirty years, among other works, you have devoted three books to a single topic, namely the concept of man in China. They are highly praised in the United States, Europe, and the Chinese speaking world. The Chinese versions, I believe, have already been published, or are in the process of being translated. Readers may be interested to know why you chose this topic and have continued with it for so long. In other words, what are the academic and historical reasons that led you to the topic?

A. My father was a founding editor of the *Journal of Aesthetics and Art Criticism*, and he was also an art museum curator. Most rooms in the house in which I grew up had pictures, statues, fabrics, or musical instruments from every continent in the world. My mother was a musician. Together with my father, they shared an interest in the music of all peoples. Some neighbors found it curious to hear Spanish guitar or Chinese opera sounds coming from our phonograph in the summer time through the open windows. But for me, it would be just one more piece of world music. And each of those pictures or fabrics on the wall was just another example of the colorful designs made by distant persons. The message that came through to me was that there is something common to all people, in this case, making art worth hanging in our house, and participating in the rituals in which the objects or musical instruments were used.

---

* English version of the Chinese, published in Harvard-Yenching Institute and Sanlian shudian eds., *Rujia yu ziyouzhuyi* (Confucianism and liberalism) (Beijing: Sanlian shudian, 2001), pp. 213–226. Slightly modified.

As a child I never made the next step, to say, "Ah, there must be a universal nature of all people." I simply focused on what people share more than on how they differ. It was not until I was in college and took a psychology course from the behaviorist B. F. Skinner, that I began to think of universal human behavior and its causes in any theoretical terms. And then eventually I concluded that that teacher was ignoring the inner life of humans in favor of their public action. There may be universal or similar aspects of all people, not simply in their visible responses to stimuli, but also in their emotions and thinking. So now I both thought about human nature in terms of universal traits, and also realized that I was criticizing a famous psychologist's view of what those traits are. So I learned that I was likely to encounter various views of human nature and should be prepared to examine them critically.

Is this topic worth spending any of my time on? The positive answer came when I noticed that, except for certain natural sciences (physics, geology, chemistry), every field of study has embedded in it assumptions about human nature. They are part of its foundation. For example, in the West, many political scientists assume that humans are capable of thinking entirely rationally when they make decisions, without the impact of the emotions on their critical reason. Of course, in this view political scientists are inheriting the position of the philosophers Herder and Hegel. Many economists assume that the main motive for any action is the individual's desire to maximize his own individual profit. So one answer to the question of the worth of the topic is that it is a good tool for discovering the basic assumptions and therefore the strength and weakness of a field of study or of an individual theory.

When I began to study about China, I began to understand a new and different reason to focus on human nature. This is that many of the Confucians justified their ethical positions by reference to human nature. Mencius was the first to startle me with this approach. It was different from some common positions in the West. In the West, religious people often justify ethical rules be appealing to the commands of God. And, of course, almost all university students are ethical relativists, believing that each person's or each society's view of right and wrong is as valid as any other's.

Q2. In the first book, *The Concept of Man in Early China* (1969), you distinguished two different meanings of equality: the descriptive and the evaluative. As a parallel, you indicated two concepts of equality:

natural equality and equality of worth. Would you explain briefly the two meanings and the two concepts? Also, I want to ask about the positions you hold on some issues relevant to these concepts. What are the respective consequences at the social and political level which the concepts helped to inspire in the West and in China? How do you explain a theoretically consistent philosophy, such as Confucianism, advocating both natural equality and social hierarchy at the same time?

A. The descriptive meaning of equality is about facts that we can see or test. It refers to common attributes with which all people are born, in terms of thinking, feeling, acting, and biological functioning. The evaluative sense is different. Normally, it is not subject to empirical testing. It carries the suggestion that people are of similar worth or deserve similar treatment. In the West this meant equal treatment before the law. But in some societies, equality of worth suggested the goal of social or status equality. This is a condition of society in which there are also minimal differences between people in the degree of respect or of the privileges that go with respect that they are shown by others. Historically, this ideal often arose as a reaction against inherited social status, in which blood line was the justification for respect and privilege. The believer in equal worth and the social egalitarian may or may not reject differences of status based on merit or societal need for certain skills or power. It all depends on what the person regards as valid or invalid arguments for going against the spirit of equal worth in the one case or of status equality in the other. For example, some believe that to be handicapped physically is a valid reason for receiving preferential parking spaces. A society may simultaneously value equal worth and also other values that may be incompatible with it. They may believe in equal treatment before the law and also in the need for preferential treatment of certain economic or ethnic groups in school admissions in order to achieve the value of a diverse student population.

Based on the findings of modern biology, I accept that humans are fairly equal in the descriptive sense. Of course, there are qualifications for people who excel in certain skills, but experience and environmental factors may play significant roles here. And there are people who are physiologically damaged. I do accept the principle of equal treatment before the law. But I do not think that social equality is a practical goal, if it means treating everyone as though their status is the same. I suspect that like many mammals, humans are by nature hierarchical. But there are two important questions: The first is, what is a good reason for assigning preferential respect and privilege to some persons, and what is a bad reason? The second is, how big should the gap be between the respect and rewards given to those with status, and to other people?

At the social and political level, there are major consequences of a viewpoint on descriptive equality that dominates in a society. In China, the Mencius belief in descriptive equality, based in the universal possession of the "four minds" dominated. As a result, anyone can be a sage. The implication was that people are perfectible through education (making exceptions for gender bias). Rulers, like parents, assume the responsibility for education. In contrast, Confucians also believe in status inequality, but their answer to the questions, "What is a good reason for assigning respect and privilege?" derives from their concept of descriptive equality. It is merit, namely those people who have perfected or educated their four minds deserve special treatment. Heredity plays a part, but a less significant part than in Japan or in Europe. Practically, this view is manifest in the civil service examination system to test merit, and in the state sponsorship of regional schools, about which the government began to get serious in the Song.

The situation in the West is very different. The dominant position, rooted in classical Greece, is opposed to natural or descriptive equality. It is that there are by birth vast differences in the reasoning ability of people and in the degree to which they are slaves to their emotions. This feeds conveniently into the Judeo-Christian religious idea of original sin, which also says that there are inborn obstructions to perfectibility. In the end, there is a wide variety of positions on what the inborn obstructions are and the consequent unchangeable differences between people. For some thinkers, original sin is found in the tendency for people to be greedy and to seek only to satisfy their own physical pleasure, unless they received the grace of God. In the modern period, the inborn obstructions might be aggressive instincts, or I.Q. differences. This position on innate differ- ences has a parallel role in providing so-called "good" reasons for status hierarchy. The rulers and other privileged people should be those with what Plato called "golden souls." Others said that high social status should go to those with the unique ability to use their critical reasoning or rationality. It was easy for families to claim that these are inherited within the lineage. In the end, the idea of equality that prevails in the modern West is "all men are created equal," which applies mainly to equal treatment under the law. This is turn has had important applications in education law, justifying attempts at some equal educational opportunity.

Q3. It seems to me that you deeply appreciate Mencius' idea of "degrees of love" and even believe that family love is the real source of altruism. However, philosophical and sociological research on China has revealed that this love often leads to a debilitating nepotism and social privilege. This phenomenon has become serious in today's China. Can I assume that Confucian ethics is partially responsible for the reality of nepotism in Chinese society, past and present? If this is the case, can I assume further that despite its important findings about the human tendency to feel degrees of love starting with family relationships, and about the family as the source of altruism, Confucian ethics failed to provide a theoretical fence to protect a good thing from going over its proper boundary?

A. Nepotism in China and elsewhere does emerge from "degrees of love." If we want to have a stable society that reduces suffering and allows everyone to pursue happiness, we must ask how to control nepotism. The answer lies in something that China is beginning to treat more seriously, but has a long way still to go: the law and oversight agencies to ensure that the laws are implemented as intended. Popular and elite attitudes of respect for law must also be developed. I believe that family members will normally give preferential treatment to their own members. This is predictable. The question then becomes, what kind of laws will protect some people from others if those others try to grab too many resources for their own family? The kinds of laws that serve this purpose are too numerous to describe here. I will just give one example: laws concerning "conflict of interest." If I am in a position of public authority and make decisions affecting other people, when there is a conflict between my private interest and that of the people who will be affected by my decision, I must withdraw from the decision making process. The same should be true of the local rules of any work organization. Managers should withdraw from decision making when there is a conflict of interest between the work organization's interest and that of their families.

Q4. It is common knowledge that individualism and liberalism have never been mainstream or dominant forces in Chinese intellectual history. Is this fact, to a certain extent, related to the idea of natural equality? What I am really interested in here is a structural relationship between several concepts: equality, freedom/liberty, and individualism. Readers may like to know, besides central totalitarianism and royal power, what was theoretically responsible for the obvious weakness of individualism and liberalism in China.

A. I will focus my reply on the question of what, other than the legacy of totalitarianism and royal power, is theoretically responsible for the weakness of individualism and liberalism in China. The answer lies in the belief that all sages or wise people think alike, and therefore, if their minds were clear, all other people would think like the sages. This is especially the case in matters of moral evaluation. The basis of this belief is the claim that all people have the same kind of moral mind, variously called by Confucians the *dao* mind or the Heavenly mind or the original mind. It differs from the physical or "human mind," in which desires may dominate. To speak of two minds, one of which is higher than the other but often unclear, is to open the door to oppressive authorities who claim to think the clear thoughts that other people would think if their minds were not so clouded by physical matter. They will teach the lesser people. Isaiah Berlin described something similar in the West in his discussion of "positive freedom" in "Two Concepts of Liberty."

Wang Yangming is widely known as an advocate of the individual as the ultimate authority, rather than the words of the classical texts being that authority. But even he fits into this pattern. Wang said, "In innate knowledge and innate ability, men and women of simple intelligence and the sage are equal. Their difference lies in the fact that the sage alone can extend [act on] his innate knowledge." The content of the mind that we all share is the same; it does not possess individual or innate differences. Its content includes, among other things, the usual Confucian values of filiality and loyalty. Twentieth century political figures who followed Wang Yangming, such as Sun Yat-sen and Chiang Kai-shek perpetuated the belief that clear headed people think the same. They enforced a system of tutelage, as Sun called it, because they held that people could not now think properly for themselves. The leadership of the Guomindang (Kuomintang) were the teachers, and the Ministry of Education was their instrument. Similar positions were dominant in the West until the nineteenth century. Before then, even that advocate of autonomy, Kant, held that all rational beings would think alike on general moral principles. He too advocated tutelage for the many people too weak willed to use their inborn reason. This opens the door to manipulation of the minds of people by their rulers "in their own interest."

In China, the political ideal sought by these believers in same-thinking was conflict avoidance through unity of thought. This political ideal had existed at least since Dong Zhongshu in the Former Han. It became known as the state of *dayitong* ("Grand Unity of Everything"). The unity includes unity of thought.

Among the things that are missing in this political ideal is the "negative freedom" that Isaiah Berlin also discussed. This is the area in which a person should be left alone to do or be what he is able to do, without obstruction from other persons. The content of that area includes, especially, thinking about ethical matters and perhaps coming up with different thoughts from those of orthodoxy or rulers. It may include ideas about problem solving, where the best solutions come when people are free to think for themselves. Western individualism includes this value of negative freedom.

Obviously, laws are needed to protect that free area and to permit the transmission of information and ideas that people think, so they can be shared and tested.

Q5. In the second book, *The Concept of Man in Contemporary China* (1977), through a comparison between Confucianism and Chinese Marxist thought, you concluded, "in some respects, the common distinction between modern and pre-modern China implies the existence of a cultural gulf that does not in fact exist." Now, over twenty-five years have passed since you wrote those words, and reforms have greatly changed Chinese society, including its intellectual climate and tendencies. Do you think that something in present day China may decisively challenge certain aspects of your conclusion? If so, what are they?

A. This remark concerned two specific aspects of Chinese culture that endured in Chinese Marxism. One was a view of the mind that, unlike the dominant Western view, refuses to separate the psychological processes of thinking, feeling, and having motives to act. This view still endures in contemporary China. The other aspect of Chinese culture found in Chinese Marxism was the acceptance of the total authority of the political center. That authority ruled through a huge bureaucracy and through trying to shape the minds of the Chinese people. This shaping was implemented by official models for the country as a whole, and by moral/political education in the schools and workplaces. There have been significant changes in the second of these aspects of the culture in the past twenty years, especially in the areas of moral/political education and in the degree of control implemented from the center over local regions.

Q6. Your third book, *Images of Human Nature: A Sung Portrait* (1988) dealt with the Neo-Confucian philosopher Zhu Xi. I was attracted to the book, first of all, by its unique and innovative method. It tried to articulate Zhu Xi's concept of man through an analysis of certain dominant structural images that Zhu employed to express his ideas. I am wondering if you would like to say something more about the method itself, its significance to international sinology, and the way you looked for its application.

A. Part of the study of human nature involves examining how people think. After years of studying Western and Chinese philosophers, I came to the hypothesis that people often think in terms of images. Some of those images are quite similar in China and the West, such as the image of light to explain knowing (to know is to be "clear, or enlightened"; not to know is to be "in the dark"). The next question is, what is the nature of those images that people use when they are explaining complicated matters. I found that in the case of Zhu Xi, the images had two functions, structural and emotive. An image structures the relations between disparate facts in the objective world to which a theory applies, calling attention to certain aspects of the relationship. For example, the plant image suggests a structure involving successive stages (as in the stages of a seasonal growth cycle). An image also elicits an emotional response to those facts. I suspect that other people, not simply Zhu Xi, also use pictorial images or analogies in the same way. When we discover the analogies they use, we can also discover the emotional content of those images and learn something about how the user intended to motivate people. We can also learn about errors in people's thinking by studying the possible differences between the item being explained and the item in the image or analogy. For example, recently it has been popular to explain the brain as a computer. There is a certain resemblance in their structures. But we must remember that there is chemistry going on in the brain, and no chemistry in the computer. So the analyst should not assume they are identical.

If we study how people think, we can draw from the history of the practice of inquiry, as I did in this third book. The textual evidence over time as to how people think is as useful in its way as archaeological material for other aspects of human behavior. Or, we can look at laboratory work on the topic. This is the subject of the laboratory studies of the neurologist Antonio Damasio, who wrote *The Feeling of What Happens: Body and Emotion in the Making of Consciousness* (New York: Harcourt Brace, 1999). He has found that thought is the flow of images. Neural patterns in the brain become images in our consciousness. An image is a mental pattern with a structure. Images are products of the interaction of us and an object that engages our organs, though that does not mean the image is a true representation of the external object. So the two subject matters, the history of works of inquiry (as in Zhu Xi) and the brain science, converge on the fact that knowing involves images in the consciousness.

Q7. When reading your recent essay, "A Modern Way to Justify Ethical Rules," the names of many contemporary authors to which you referred have never appeared in your books before. It can be regarded as a new exploration in the field of human nature. Consequently, does this new study result in substantial revision of the major points of view in the three books mentioned above?

A. For a long time I have believed that much knowledge is interrelated. Of course, many of China's great Neo-Confucian scholars also believed this, and it helped to motivate the creation of encyclopedias. For people interested in human nature, evolutionary biology and evolutionary psychology offer the newest knowledge available. So someone who has read the earlier works of philosophers, both Western and Chinese, can also learn much from these new sciences. Note the title of the book by the biologist Edward O. Wilson: *Consilience: The Unity of Knowledge* (New York: Knopf, 1998). Much of the information comes from gene studies, whether of worms, insects, fish, or humans. We share much of our genome with these creatures.

So I think we can find in the new science suggestions about what topics in the works of the earlier figures are insightful and which may best be ignored. For example, the new biology reveals that altruism emerges as a matter of reciprocity. Altruistic behavior may benefit some other individual(s), not necessarily close kin, while costing something to the organism providing the benefits. But in the long term, the benefactor or his kin who carry some of his genes will benefit, as the favor is returned in the future. (For the biologist, benefit and cost are measured in terms of reproduction of the individual's genes and their survival.) Knowing this, I would have dealt with a crucial weakness in Confucianism in a different way. The weakness lies in the absence of any clear Confucian answer to this question: How can people ensure that *ren* (humane, altruistic behavior) extends beyond the family? Confucians do not have much obvious theoretical discussion of this matter. But buried in their texts is an awareness of reciprocity (*shu*) as an important value. And the term *de* (as in *dao-de*) or virtue is often defined in terms of reciprocity. Those who have excellent *de* and are kind to others, will get (*de* meaning to get) good fortune or something desirable in return. So I would have encouraged the Confucian writers to tie these discussions of reciprocity into their already rich writings on education, so as to sensitize the individual through education that behaving with *ren* has its own rewards. This gives a reason to be humane beyond the family.

I would also have focused more on the role of law as a necessary tool to ensure harmonious social relations and stability. Where Mencian "degreed love" is taught, there must be laws to reduce nepotism by controlling conflict of interest, and by providing education and nurturance to those with inadequate or no family resources.

Q8. The doctrine of "free will" is central to much Western philosophy, especially since the time of Saint Augustine (354–430) There is no similar quantity of discussion about free choice in the history of Chinese philosophy. Why is this so?

A. In the West, the topic of "free will" is linked to some core Christian religious doctrines. Augustine wrote *On the Free Choice of the Will* to clear God of blame for evil be showing that free will in man is the cause of evil. The problem was that religious doctrine required God to be omnipotent, all knowing, and good. If He is all those things, why does He allow evil to occur? The answer is that God gives humans free choice. So the individual has the power to choose and hence to be wrong and do evil. God is therefore absolved from responsibility for evil. Evil resides in the will, which is the place of choice.

According to Zhu Xi, evil has always existed because of the material dust that darkens the self-bright light within the human mind, present as the *li* or principles. This dust obstructs knowledge and action according to knowledge. Because evil has always been around in the material constitution of the world or in the relation of *li* to *qi*, no god is disgraced by its presence. So the central issue for Zhu Xi is not where to assign responsibility, and blame or praise, for doing evil or for avoiding it. Instead, the issue is: Recognizing that knowledge is defective, how do we clear the mind ("polish the mirror" or "clear the dirt from the muddy water")? His answer is self-cultivation and the teachings of Confucian authorities within the school of *daoxue*. In other words, his focus is on the nature of the human mind and on the education that can clear it. Biographically speaking, Zhu Xi became a model educator, building academies, as well as serving nine years as an official.

Another factor pertains to the different psychological portraits of the mind in the West and in China. As I said, the Western thinkers assigned evil to the will, which they treated as part of the mind, whereas Zhu Xi assigns it to the dense *qi* in the world and in the human mind. The Westerners believed that the mind has three parts, reason, emotions, and will. This tripartite division was originally influenced by the political analogy from Greece of three classes of people in society. The social analogy was applied to the mind. In contrast, Zhu Xi's view of the mind has only two aspects, the *dao* mind and the human mind, or, to use the social analogy, the ruler and ruled. Whereas in the West, the "will" became a thing with a place of its own, the terms that Zhu Xi uses in talking about choosing do not refer to a separate thing, like a Western "will." They include *yi* (intention, volition), which refers to the "out thrust of the mind." They also include *quan*, meaning to weigh in a scale; choosing is also not done by a separate thing or part of the mind.

Finally, as for the consequences of doing evil, again there are differences that make the issue of free will central to the Western thinker and of less immediacy to the Chinese. The Western individual who makes a wrong choice and does evil can expect blame and punishment from God or God's agents among the priests or kings. But for Zhu Xi, failure to remove obstacles to understanding carries negative consequences that are built into the natural system. These are a sense of mental unbalance, unease, and separation from others. The individual may suffer these long after he does the bad deed. The time between committing an act and meeting its consequences may be long, perhaps generations. So bad deeds are inauspicious, to use the language of divination. They are not evil in the religious sense of violation of God's rules.

In the modern West, the scientific revolution and the machine age suggested to some religious people that humans, like other things made of matter, might be simply governed by the laws of the motion of atoms. They feared material determinism once again. Humans may not be free. So, like their ancestors who opposed ancient atomists such as Democritus, they intensified the goal of again grounding morality in free will. They would have been better off grounding it in human nature, as Mencius did and as Mill did.

Any Chinese who wishes to retain a doctrine of free choice can simply disconnect it from all the Christian theological doctrines and save himself trouble. Free choice can exist apart from an omnipotent God, a thing called "the will," and from blaming.

Q9. Finally, what is the fate of Confucianism as a major social and ethical school of thought in this new century? In other words, are there any elements in Confucianism which can positively influence world society?

A. If advocates of Confucianism learn from the new sciences and modify their assumptions accordingly, I see Confucianism as having a healthy life in the new century. Confucianism already has three central teachings from which anyone interested in ethics can learn. One is that each individual carries as part of his identity certain role relations: husband-wife, daughter-parent, older sibling-younger sibling. Some of our moral duties are involved in these relations. So, ethics does not only involve the individual but also the individual in relation to those with whom he has close bonds. Second, the emotions are tightly bound up with our knowing and our motivation. Any ethic that ignores them (including familial emotions) will be viewed as impractical and alienating. Third, humaneness or altruism begins in the family, where it must then be nurtured.

But there are also a few Confucian teachings that must be ignored. One is the idea from state Confucianism that the ruler is the father of the people and the teacher of the people. This helped to produce the value of "the great unity of everything," including uniformity of thought. It also helped to reinforce a dislike of specialists in the law, because they were seen as third persons, coming between the ruler/father and his children.

But the law is needed to protect people against each other and against their rulers, when any of those others behave too selfishly. And pluralism is preferable to uniformity of thought because it works. It produces the greatest variety of proposals as to how to solve problems, and in variety lies the promise of finding the best solutions.

May 1, 2000

Appendix:
Donald Munro's Key Works

The Concept of Man in Early China. Stanford: Stanford University Press, 1969.

The Concept of Man in Contemporary China. Ann Arbor: The University of Michigan Press, 1977.

Images of Human Nature: A Sung Portrait. Princeton: Princeton University Press, 1988.

The Imperial Style of Inquiry in Twentieth-century China. Ann Arbor: Center for Chinese Studies, The University of Michigan, 1996.

Individualism and Holism: Studies in Confucian and Taoist Values. Ann Arbor: Center for Chinese Studies, The University of Michigan, 1985. (edited work)

Notes

Preface

1. John Alcock, *The Triumph of Sociobiology* (Oxford: Oxford University Press, 2001), p. 53.
2. Matt Ridley, *Nature Via Nurture* (New York: Harper Collins, 2003), pp. 244–245. Also Niko Tinbergen, "On the Aims and Methods of Ethology," *Zeitschrift fur Tierpsychologie*, 20 (1963), pp. 410–463.
3. William R. Clark and Michael Grunstein, *Are We Hardwired? The Role of Genes in Human Behavior* (Oxford: Oxford University Press, 2000), p. 160.
4. Antonio Damasio, *Looking for Spinoza: Joy, Sorrow, and the Feeling Brain* (New York: Harcourt, 2003), p. 165.
5. Edward O. Wilson, *Consilience: The Unity of Knowledge* (New York: Knopf, 1998), pp. 169, 310.
6. Damasio, pp. 39, 47.

Introduction

1. This article is based on two Chinese essays: "A Great Scholar in the Study of Comparative Philosophy and Human Nature: Donald Munro's Studies on the History of Chinese Philosophy," in *Studies of China by Western Sinologists* (Xifang Hanxuejia lun Zhongguo), ed. Charles Fu (Taipei: Chung Cheng Co., 1993), pp. 173–203, trans. Terre Fisher; "Opening a New Frontier for Chinese Philosophy: An Introduction to Donald Munro's Academic Work," in pamphlet for *Ch'ien Mu Lecture in History and Culture* (Hong Kong: New Asia College, The Chinese University of Hong Kong, 2003), pp. 1–8, trans. Donald Munro.
2. The biographical section here relies on information from correspondence with Professor Munro and his former student, Professor Robert Eno, at Indiana University.
3. Roger Trigg, *Understanding Social Science* (Oxford: Blackwell, 1989).
4. Professor Munro would like to take this opportunity to express his thanks to his former student Dr. Sin-Yee Chan. She helped to clarify this meaning in contemporary Western ethics.
5. See *The Concept of Man in Early China* (Stanford: Stanford University Press, 1969), p. 179, note.
6. *Analects*, 17.2. For a different translation, see *Confucius the Analects*, trans. D. C. Lau (Harmondsworth; New York: Penguin Books, 1979), p. 143.

7. *Mencius*, 6A.7, trans. D. C. Lau (Harmondsworth; New York: Penguin Books, 1979), p. 164.

8. *Xunzi*, 9, "Wang zhi" (Kingly regulations). For complete translation, see *Basic Writings of Hsun Tzu*, trans. Burton Watson (New York: Columbia University Press, 1963), p. 33.

9. Mozi, "Shang xian" (Honoring the worthy). *Mozi*, 8, from *Mo Tzu: Basic Writings*, trans. Burton Watson (New York: Columbia University Press, 1963), pp. 20–21.

10. Han Feizi, "You du" (Having limits), from *The Complete Works of Han Fei Tzu*, trans. W. K. Liao (London: Probsthain, 1959), vol. 1, p. 45.

11. See *The Concept of Man in Early China*, pp. 2–4.

12. The content of this paragraph and the following comes mostly from *The Concept of Man in Early China*, pp. 18–21, 179–182. Wherever Munro's book quotes from sources in other languages, it refers to the original work; to save space I do not repeat those source of citations here.

13. The contents of this section come from *The Concept of Man in Contemporary China* (Ann Arbor: The University of Michigan Press, 1977), chapter 2. The paragraphs above are quoted from page 26.

14. *Chuanxi lu*, II.168, "Da Ouyang Chongyi." See Wang Yangming, *Instructions for Practical Living and Other Neo-Confucian Writings by Wang Yang-ming*, trans. Wing-tsit Chan (New York: Columbia University Press, 1963), p. 150.

15. Mengzi, "Gaozi." *Mencius*, 6A.7, trans. D. C. Lau (Harmondsworth: Penguin, 1970), p. 164.

16. Wang Yangming, III.288, trans. Wing-tsit Chan, p. 228.

17. Ibid., I.5, trans. Wing-tsit Chan, p. 10.

18. Professor Munro stresses that it was Professor D. C. Lau who first distinguished these meanings for "right" and "wrong."

19. *Yishu* (Posthumous works), 15. In Cheng Yi, *Er Cheng quanshu* (The complete works of the two Cheng brothers), *Sibu beiyao* (Comprehensive collection of the four categories) ed., 15.16b.

20. Mao Zedong, "Shijianlun" (On practice). For a different translation, see *Five Essays on Philosophy* (Beijing: Foreign Languages Press, 1977), pp. 2–3.

21. In recent years some American philosophers have opposed the sort of theory that demarcates the meaning of facts from that of emotions.

22. *Analects*, 13.18. For a different translation, see *Analects*, trans. D. C. Lau, p. 121.

23. *Chunqiu Zuozhuan* (Zuo's Commentary on *The Spring and Autumn Annals*), Duke Zhao 14. In *Chunqiu Zuozhuan Zhu*, ed. Yang Bojun (Beijing: Zhonghua shuju, 1981), vol. 4, p. 1367.

Chapter 1

1. I first discussed the difference between natural equality and evaluative

equality of worth in my book, *The Concept of Man in Early China* (Stanford: Stanford University Press, 1969), chapter 1.

2. "*Wude bubao.*" See *The Book of Odes*, trans. Bernard Karlgren (Stockholm: Museum of Far Eastern Antiquities, 1950), p. 218.

3. Edward O. Wilson, *Consilience: The Unity of Knowledge* (New York: Knopf, 1998), p. 253.

4. Robert Wright, *The Moral Animal* (New York: Vintage, 1994), p. 201.

5. Robert L. Trivers, "The Evolution of Reciprocal Altruism," *Quarterly Review of Biology*, 46 (1971), p. 43.

6. Peter Singer, ed., *Ethics* (Oxford: Oxford University Press, 1994).

7. Michael Specter, "The Dangerous Philosopher," *The New Yorker*, September 6 (1999), p. 55.

8. Steven Pinker, *How the Mind Works* (New York: Norton, 1997), p. 44.

9. Randy Thornhill and Craig T. Palmer, *A Natural History of Rape: Biological Bases of Sexual Coercion* (Cambridge, MA: M.I.T. Press, 2001).

10. Raimond Gaita, *A Common Humanity* (London: Routledge, 1998), pp. 73–74.

11. *Mencius*, 7A.1.

12. Zhu Xi, *Zuzi quanshu* (Complete works of Master Zhu), facsimile reprint of the 1885 reprint of the 1715 ed., 2 vols. (Taipei: Kuangxue she, 1977), 43.25b–26a (2:980–981). Reference is to the *zhuan* and page in the original, followed in parentheses by volume and page in the modern edition cited here.

13. See Victor H. Mair, "Language and Ideology in the Written Popularizations of the *Sacred Edict*," in *Popular Culture in Late Imperial China*, eds. David Johnson et al. (Los Angeles: University of California Press, 1985), pp. 325ff.

14. Gaita, p. 261.

15. *Mencius*, 1A.7, from *The Chinese Classics*, trans. James Legge (Hong Kong: Hong Kong University Press, 1960), vol. 2, *The Works of Mencius*.

16. Steven Pinker, *The Blank Slate* (New York: Viking, 2002), p. 169.

17. Alexis de Tocqueville, *Democracy in America*, ed. J. P. Mayer, trans. George Lawrence (New York: Doubleday, 1969), part II, p. 436.

18. Pinker, *The Blank Slate*, pp. 180, 185.

19. Emily Hannum and Albert Park, "Educating China's Rural Children in the 21st Century," *Harvard China Review*, III.2 (Spring 2002), p. 12. Also, *New York Times*, August 1 (2004), pp. 1, 6.

20. John Plamenatz, "Equality of Opportunity," in *The Concept of Equality*, ed. W. T. Blackstone (Minneapolis: Burgess Publishing Co., 1969), p. 93.

21. Randolph M. Nesse, "Natural Selection and the Capacity for Subjective Commitment," in *Evolution and the Capacity for Commitment*, ed. Randolph M. Nesse (New York: Russell Sage Foundation, 2001), p. 30. See also pp. 16, 18, 27.

Chapter 2

1. I first discussed these matters in my book, *Images of Human Nature: A Sung*

Portrait (Princeton: Princeton University Press, 1988), chapters 3 and 4.

2. *Zhuzi yulei* (Classified conversations of Master Zhu Xi), reprint of the 1473 ed., 8 vols. (Taipei: Zhengzhong shuju, 1962), hereafter cited as ZZYL. The first set of numbers indicates the *zhuan* and page, the second set gives the volume number and consecutive pagination. Hence, here ZZYL, 15.17a; 1:543.

3. *Zhuzi quanshu* (Complete works of Master Zhu), facsimile reprint of the 1885 reprint of the 1715 ed., 2 vols. (Taipei: Kuangxue she, 1977), hereafter cited as ZZQS. References are to the *zhuan* and page in the original, followed in parentheses by volume and page in the modern edition cited here. Hence, here, ZZQS, 44.12b (2:993). Also in ZZYL, 98.11b; 6:4059.

4. Cheng Yi, in *Reflections on Things at Hand*, trans. W. T. Chan (New York: Columbia University Press, 1967), p. 45.

5. *Cuiyan* (Pure words), 1.2b, in Cheng Hao and Cheng Yi, *Er Cheng quanshu* (Complete works of the two Chengs), *Sibu beiyao* ed.

6. ZZYL, 20.23a; 2:823. Filiality is the root of practicing humaneness. It cannot be treated as the root of humaneness itself, because humaneness is principle (*li*), the hidden root of all virtue.

7. ZZQS, 45.4b (2:1007). For growth stages caused by the mind of heaven and earth, and present in all living things, see 44.7b (2:990).

8. Ibid., 44.10b (2:992).

9. ZZYL, 74.19b; 5:3078.

10. Ibid., 62.25b; 4:2456.

11. *New York Times*, September 10 (1998), p. A20, in Jefferson's letter to the Danbury Baptist Association.

12. ZZQS, 46.4a (2:1017).

13. ZZYL, 20.23a; 2:823.

14. Ibid., 20.13b; 2:804.

15. Ibid., 64.16a; 4:2567.

16. Zhu Xi, *Xiaoxue jiju* (Collected commentaries on the Elementary Learning), *Sibu beiyao* ed., 6.3b–4a. In his commentary on *Analects*, 6.3, Zhu says that people living in the same neighborhood should help each other.

17. Zhu Xi, *Huaian xiansheng Zhu Wengong wenji* (Collection of literary works of Master Zhu), *Sibu congkan* ed., vol. 12, 25.12a.

18. For the Hymes reference, see my *Images of Human Nature*, pp. 148, 303.

19. Robert P. Hymes, "Prominence and Power in Sung China: The Local Elite of Fu-chou, Chiang-his," Ph.D. dissertation, University of Pennsylvania, 1979, p. 279.

20. Patricia B. Ebrey, *Family and Property in Sung China* (Princeton: Princeton University Press, 1983), pp. 158, 166.

21. I owe this insight to discussion following this lecture at the Philosophy Department of New Asia College, The Chinese University of Hong Kong, February, 2003.

Chapter 3

1. Some of this material is derived from chapters 3 and 5 of my book, *The Imperial Style of Inquiry in Twentieth-Century China: The Emergence of New Approaches* (Ann Arbor: Center for Chinese Studies, University of Michigan, 1996).

2. *Analects*, 4.17.

3. Ibid., 8.2, from *The Chinese Classics*, trans. James Legge (Hong Kong: Hong Kong University Press, 1960), vol. 1, p. 208.

4. *The Great Learning*, ix, 8.9, from Legge, vol. 1, p. 372.

5. *Analects*, 2.3, from Legge, vol. 1, p. 146.

6. Discussed in my book, *The Concept of Man in Contemporary China* (Michigan Classics in Chinese Studies; Ann Arbor: Center for Chinese Studies, University of Michigan, 2000, reprinted from the 1977 version published by University of Michigan Press), p. 137.

7. Zhu Xi, *Huaian xiansheng Zhu Wengong wenji* (Collection of literary works of Master Zhu), *Sibu congkan* ed., vol. 33, 70.24a.

8. Ray Huang, *1587, A Year of No Significance: The Ming Dynasty in Decline* (New Haven: Yale University Press, 1981), p. 89. See also pp. 63, 77, 90.

9. Yang Jianye, *Ma Yinchu zhuan* (Biography of Ma Yinchu) (Beijing: Zhongguo qingnian chubanshe, 1986), p. 168; and Jiang Shan, *Maersasi "Renkou lun" he "Xin renkou lun" de piping* (Critique of Malthus's "Theory of Population" and of "A New Theory of Population") (Shanghai: Shanghai renmin chubanshe, 1958), pp. 58, 60–63.

10. Yang Jianye, pp. 238–239.

11. "Song Zhenming jiu 'Bohai erhao' zuanjingchuan fanchen shigu jiantao" (Song Zhenming's self-criticism concerning the Bohai No. 2 platform), *Xinhua yuekan*, 8 (1980), p. 71; and "Shenke de jiaoxun" (A profound lesson), *Xinhua yuekan*, 8 (1980), p. 69.

12. Guo Zhan, "The Course of Human Subjectivity," *Social Sciences in China*, 4 (1987), p. 209.

13. Tze-wan Kwan, "Subject and Person as Two Self-images of Modern Man: Some Cross Cultural Perspectives," paper presented at the International Conference "Issues Confronting the Post-European World," November, 2002, Prague.

14. Examples are drawn from *Zhongguo qingnian* (China youth), 5 (1980), pp. 2–5; 7 (1980), pp. 4–6; 1 (1988), pp. 2–5; and 9 (1992), pp. 12–13.

15. See Munro, *The Imperial Style of Inquiry*, pp. 99–106.

16. Wang Yangming, *Instructions for Practical Living and Other Neo-Confucian Writings by Wang Yang-ming*, trans. Wing-tsit Chan (New York: Columbia University Press, 1963), II.139, p. 108.

17. John Stuart Mill, *On Liberty* (New York: Library of Liberal Arts/Bobbs-Merrill, 1956), pp. 69–70.

18. Antonio Damasio, *Looking for Spinoza* (New York: Harcourt, 2003), pp. 148–149.

Chapter 4

1. Richard Rorty, *Truth and Progress: Philosophical Papers* (Cambridge: Cambridge University Press, 1998), vol. 3, pp. 169–170.
2. Edward O. Wilson notes, "Where cultural relativism has been initiated to negate belief in hereditary behavioral differences among ethnic groups … it was turned against the idea of a unified human nature guided by heredity." In Edward O. Wilson, *Consilience: The Unity of Knowledge* (New York: Knopf, 1998), p. 185. Hardback edition. Pagination different from paper edition. See also Robert Wright on the "well-meaning bias" of Boasians, in *The Moral Animal* (New York: Vintage, 1994), p. 237.
3. *Mencius*, 3A.4.
4. Ibid., 7A.45.
5. Ibid., 7A.15.
6. Wilson, p. 253.
7. Ibid., p. 169.
8. *The Book of Odes*, trans. Bernard Karlgren (Stockholm: Museum of Far Eastern Antiquities, 1950), *Yi* 6, p. 218.
9. *Analects*, 15.23.
10. Robert L. Trivers, "The Evolution of Reciprocal Altruism," *Quarterly Review f Biology*, 46 (1971), p. 39. See also Robert Wright, *Non-Zero: The Logic of Human Destiny* (New York: Pantheon, 2000), p. 294.
11. Trivers, p. 43.
12. Wright, *The Moral Animal*, p. 201.
13. Matt Ridley, *The Origins of Virtue: Human Instincts and the Evolution of Cooperation* (New York: Penguin, 1996), p. 63; Steven Pinker, *How the Mind Works* (New York: Norton, 1997), p. 503; Wright, *The Moral Animal*, p. 193. I have discussed this and the following few paragraphs in my Foreword to the reprint edition of *The Concept of Man in Contemporary China* (Michigan Classics in Chinese Studies; Ann Arbor: Center for Chinese Studies, University of Michigan, 2000), pp. viii-ix.
14. *New York Times*, September 25 (2001), p. D3.
15. Antonio R. Damasio, *The Feeling of What Happens: Body and Emotion in the Making of Consciousness* (New York: Harcourt Brace, 1999), pp. 40–41.
16. Ibid., p. 286.
17. Pinker, p. 370.
18. Ibid., p. 373.
19. Wilson, p. 106.
20. Ibid., p. 113.
21. Trivers, pp. 49–50.
22. Ibid., p. 48.

23. Ibid., p. 50.
24. Matt Ridley, *Nature Via Nature* (New York: Harper, 2003).
25. William R. Clark and Michael Grunstein, *Are We Hardwired? The Role of Genes in Human Behavior* (Oxford: Oxford University Press, 2000), p. 155.
26. Ridley, pp. 129–130.
27. Evelyn Fox Keller and Elisabeth A. Lloyd, *Keywords in Evolutionary Biology* (Cambridge, MA: Harvard University Press, 1999), p. 255.
28. Ridley, p. 145.
29. Clark and Grunstein, p. 269.
30. Pinker, pp. 58, 424.
31. Steven Pinker, *The Blank Slate* (New York: Viking, 2002), pp. 180, 185.
32. Antonio Damasio, *Looking for Spinoza* (New York: Harcourt, 2003), pp. 52, 80. Damasio is a neurologist.
33. Wilson, pp. 169 (parental investment), 169, 205, 258 (altruism), 193 (avoidance of incest), 253 (cooperation), and 171 (contract making).
34. Pinker, *The Blank Slate*, pp. 169 and 164.
35. *Analects*, 2.3, from *The Chinese Classics*, trans. James Legge (Hong Kong: Hong Kong University Press, 1960), vol. 1, p. 146.
36. See V. S. Ramachandran, "Mirror Neurons and Imitation Learning as the Driving Force behind the 'Great Leap Forward' in Human Evolution," retrieved March 27, 2004 from http://www.edge.org/3rd_culture/ranachandran/ramachandran_index.html
37. Bruce Bower, "Repeat After Me: Imitation is the Sincerest Form of Perception," *Science News*, May 24 (2003), p. 2.
38. John Alcock, *The Triumph of Sociobiology* (Oxford: Oxford University Press, 2001), p. 201.
39. Randolph M. Nesse, ed., *Evolution and the Capacity for Commitment* (New York: Russell Sage Foundation, 2001).

Chapter 5

1. Cited in *Harpers*, May (1990), p. 34.
2. Edward O. Wilson, *Consilience: The Unity of Knowledge* (New York: Knopf, 1998), p. 164.
3. See the discussion by Carlin Romano, "Rortyism for Beginners," *The Nation*, July 27/August 3 (1998). Romano is discussing the second set of essays in Richard Rorty, *Truth and Progress: Philosophical Papers* (Cambridge: Cambridge University Press, 1998), vol. 3.
4. Steven Levy, "Dr. Edelman's Brain," *The New Yorker*, May 2 (1994), p. 68.
5. *Mencius*, 7A.1, trans. D. C. Lau, *Mencius* (Harmondsworth: Penguin, 1976), p. 182.
6. *Mencius*, 1A.7, 2A.6.
7. Ibid., 4A.12 and also various passages about Heaven making the crucial decisions about who should rule.

8. E. O. Wilson, *Consilience*, p. 249.
9. *Mencius*, 2A.6, trans. Lau, p. 82.
10. Primo Levi, *Survival in Auschwitz and the Reawakening, Two Memoirs* (New York: Summit Books, 1965), p. 86.
11. Ibid., p. 160.
12. *Mencius*, 6A.7, trans. Lau, p. 164.
13. Ibid., 6A.1, 2, trans. Lau, p. 160.
14. Ibid.
15. Ibid., 3A.4, trans. Lau, p. 103.
16. Ibid., 1A.6, trans. Lau, p. 54.
17. Ibid., 4A.2, trans. Lau, p. 118.
18. Ibid., 6A.7.
19. E. O. Wilson, *Consilience*, p. 106.
20. Ibid., p. 113.
21. Ibid., p. 179.
22. Ibid., p. 253. Also, Edward O. Wilson, "The Biological Basis of Morality," *The Atlantic Monthly*, April (1998), p. 59.
23. *Mencius*, 3A.4 and 7B.24.
24. Ibid., 7A.45.
25. Ibid., 7A.15.
26. E. O. Wilson, *Consilience*, p. 164.
27. Ibid., p. 169.
28. Ibid., p. 205.
29. James Q. Wilson, *The Moral Sense* (New York: The Free Press, 1993), p. 46.
30. Ibid., p. 8.
31. Ibid., p. 11.
32. Ibid., p. 43.
33. Ibid., p. 19.
34. Ibid., p. 25.
35. E. O. Wilson, *Consilience*, p. 253.
36. Elie Wiesel, *Memoirs All Rivers Run to the Sea* (New York: Knopf, 1995), p. 78.
37. E. O. Wilson, "The Biological Basis of Morality," p. 59.
38. *Mencius*, 3A.4, trans. Lau, p. 101.

Chapter 6

1. *Mencius*, 7A.1, trans. D. C. Lau (Middlesex: Penguin, 1976), p. 182.
2. Melville J. Herskovits, "Ethical Relativism," in *Reason and Responsibility*, ed. Joel Feinberg (Belmont: Wadsworth, 1989), p. 471.
3. Edward O. Wilson, *Consilience: The Unity of Knowledge* (New York: Knopf, 1998), chapter 11: "Ethics and Religion," pp. 238–265. Hardback edition. Pagination different from paper edition.

4. Mao Zedong, *Talks at the Yen'an Forum on Art and Literature* (Beijing: Foreign Languages Press, 1960), pp. 36–37.

5. Richard Rorty, *Truth and Progress: Philosophical Papers* (Cambridge: Cambridge University Press, 1998), vol. 3.

6. Antonio R. Damasio, *The Feeling of What Happens: Body and Emotion in the Making of Consciousness* (New York: Harcourt Brace, 1999), p. 71.

7. Ibid., p. 78.

8. Robert Wright, *The Moral Animal* (New York: Vintage, 1994).

9. Ibid., p. 334.

10. Peter Singer, ed., *Ethics* (Oxford: Oxford University Press, 1994).

11. John Plamenatz, *Man and Society*, (New York: McGraw-Hill, 1969), pp. 2, 22.

12. *Analects*, 1.2.

13. *Mencius*, 7A.15, trans. Lau, p. 184.

14. Ibid., 1A.7, trans. Lau, p. 56.

15. Wilson, p. 169.

16. Robert L. Trivers, "The Evolution of Reciprocal Altruism," *Quarterly Review of Biology*, 46 (1971), p. 39.

17. Wright, p. 201.

18. Trivers, p. 38.

19. Wright, p. 193. Matt Ridley, *The Origins of Virtue: Human Instincts and the Evolution of Cooperation* (New York: Penguin, 1996), p. 63.

20. Wilson, p. 253.

21. J. Smart and Bernard Williams, *Utilitarianism: For and Against* (Cambridge: Cambridge University Press, 1973).

22. Wilson, p. 113.

23. H. L. A. Hart, "Review of Bernard Williams, *Ethics and the Limits of Philosophy*," *The New York Review of Books*, July 17 (1986), p. 50.

24. Damasio, p. 286.

25. Wilson, p. 106.

26. Steven Pinker, *How the Mind Works* (New York: Norton, 1997), p. 373.

27. Trivers, pp. 48–50.

28. Michael Specter, "The Dangerous Philosopher," *The New Yorker*, September 6 (1999), p. 55.

29. Pinker, p. 44.

30. Matt Ridley, *Genome: The Autobiography of a Species in 23 Chapters* (New York: Harper Collins, 1999), p. 312.

Chapter 7

1. Matt Ridley, *Nature Via Nurture* (New York: HarperCollins, 2002).

2. I first examined these matters in "The Malleability of Man in Chinese Marxism," *The China Quarterly*, 48 (October–November 1971), pp. 609–640, and in *The Concept of Man in Contemporary China* (Ann Arbor:

University of Michigan Press, 1977; reprinted as Michigan Classics in Chinese Studies, No. 3, 2000), chapter 3.

3. Cited in *The Concept of Man in Contemporary China*, p. 58.

4. Ibid., p. 59.

5. Ibid., p. 59.

6. Ibid., pp. 64–68.

7. Steven Pinker, *The Blank Slate* (New York: Viking, 2002), p. 5.

8. Ridley, p. 205.

9. Ullica Segerstrale, *Defenders of the Truth: The Battle for Science in the Sociology Debate and Beyond* (Oxford: Oxford University Press, 2000), pp. 142, 182, 248, 391.

10. John Alcock, *The Triumph of Sociobiology* (Oxford: Oxford University Press, 2001), p. 153.

11. Ibid., p. 130. Citation about Benzer is in Jonathan Weiner, *Time, Love, Memory: A Great Biologist and His Quest for the Origins of Behavior* (New York: Knopf, 1999), pp. 177–178.

12. William R. Clark and Michael Grunstein, *Are We Hardwired? The Role of Genes in Human Behavior* (Oxford: Oxford University Press, 2000), p. 155.

13. Ridley, pp. 129–130.

14. Evelyn Fox Keller and Elisabeth A. Lloyd, *Keywords in Evolutionary Biology* (Cambridge, MA: Harvard University Press, 1999), p. 255.

15. Ridley, p. 145.

16. Clark and Grunstein, p. 269.

17. Steven Pinker, *How the Mind Works* (New York: Norton, 1997), pp. 58, 424.

18. Pinker, *The Blank Slate*, pp. 180, 185.

19. Antonio Damasio, *Looking for Spinoza* (New York: Harcourt, 2003), pp. 52, 80. Damasio is a neurologist.

20. Edward O. Wilson, *Consilience: The Unity of Knowledge* (New York: Knopf, 1998), pp. 169 (parental investment), 169, 205, 258 (altruism), 193 (avoidance of incest), 253 (cooperation), and 171 (contract making).

21. Pinker, *The Blank Slate*, pp. 169 and 164.

22. Alcock, p. 201.

Chapter 9

1. Wm. Theodore de Bary, *The Message of the Mind in Neo-Confucianism* (New York: Columbia University Press, 1989).

2. Lionel M. Jensen, *Manufacturing Confucianism* (Durham: Duke University Press, 1998), p. 140.

3. Ibid., p. 145.

4. Jared Diamond, *Guns, Germs, and Steel: The Fates of Human Societies* (New York: Norton, 1997).

5. Ibid., p. 286.

6. Ibid. See all of chapter 14, pp. 265–292.

7. Edward O. Wilson, *Consilience: The Unity of Knowledge* (New York: Knopf, 1998), p. 164. I have already discussed the material in this and the next paragraph in "Mencius and an Ethics of the New Century," in *Mencius: Contexts and Interpretations*, ed. Alan K. L. Chan (Honolulu: University of Hawaii Press, 2002), pp. 305–315.

8. James Q. Wilson, *The Moral Sense* (New York: The Free Press, 1993), p. 19.

9. E. O. Wilson, *Consilience*, p. 253. Also, Edward O. Wilson, "The Biological Basis of Morality," *The Atlantic Monthly*, April (1998), p. 59.

10. *Mencius*, 7A.45.

11. Ibid., 7A.15.

12. E. O. Wilson, *Consilience*, p. 169.

13. Jensen, p. 281.

14. Ibid., p. 271.

15. *Analects*, 2.1.

Selected Glossary

Chan	禪	Ma Yinchu	馬寅初
Chen Lifu	陳立夫	*nengdongxing*	能動性
cheng	誠	*qingguan*	清官
Cheng Yi	程頤	*ren*	仁
Cui Shu	崔述	*shenjiao sheng yu*	身教勝於言教
Da Yu mo	大禹謨	*yanjiao*	
Dagao	大誥	Shenming ting	申明亭
daode	道德	*shexue*	社學
daoxue	道學	*shi*	士
Daqing	大慶	*shifei zhi xin*	是非之心
dayitong	大一統	*shili*	實理
de	德／得	Shunzhi	順治
Dong Zhongshu	董仲舒	Shuowen	說文
duli sikao	獨立思考	*shuyuan*	書院
fengqi yinzi	封妻蔭子	Sima Guang	司馬光
fumuguan	父母官	Sima Tan	司馬談
gandong	感動	Taizhou	泰州
ganying	感應	Tang Junyi	唐君毅
gong	公	*tiandao*	天道
gongfu	工夫	*tianli*	天理
Gu Jiegang	顧頡剛	Tiantai	天台
guagou danwei	掛鉤單位	*tiren*	體仁
He Lin	賀麟	*tongqingxin*	同情心
He Xinyin	何心隱	Wang Anshi	王安石
Huang-Lao	黃老	Wang Gen	王艮
hui	會	Wang Guowei	王國維
jingshi	經世	Wang Renshu	王任叔
jingtian	井田	Wang Yangming	王陽明
Lei Feng	雷鋒	*weifa*	未發
li	理	*wu de bu bao*	無德不報
Li Dazhao	李大釗	*xian*	縣
Li Zhi	李贄	*xiangyinjiuli*	鄉飲酒禮
liangzhi	良知	*xiangyue*	鄉約
Liu Xiaogan	劉笑敢	*Xin renkou lun*	新人口論
Lu Jiuyuan	陸九淵	Xiong Shili	熊十力
Lü Buwei	呂不韋	*xuanze ziji de*	選擇自己的
Lüshi chunqiu	呂氏春秋	*qiantu*	前途

yi	義		*zhenru*	真儒
yifa	已發		*zhi*	志
yixue	義學		Zhouli	周禮
youjiao wulei	有教無類		Zhu Xi	朱熹
Yuan Cai	袁采		Zhuangzi	莊子
Zhang Zai	張載		*zhutixing*	主體性
zhao	照		*zizhi*	自治
Zhaogong	昭公		*zizhu*	自主

Index